ENEMY
ACCESS
DENIED

JOHN BEVERE

Charisma
HOUSE
A STRANG COMPANY

Library of Congress Cataloging-in-Publication Data

Bevere, John.

  Enemy access denied / John Bevere.

      p. cm.

  Includes bibliographical references.

  ISBN 1-59185-960-3 (paper back)

  1. Spiritual warfare. I. Title.

  BV4509.5.B49 2006

  235'.4--dc22

                                        2006004188

Previously published as *The Devil's Door* by Charisma House,
ISBN 0-88419-442-6, copyright © 1996.

06 07 08 09 10—9 8 7 6 5 4 3 2 1

Printed in the United States of America

ACKNOWLEDGMENTS

I would like to acknowledge and express gratitude for the following people who have had an impact on my life:

My parents, John and Kay Bevere, for living a godly life before me.

My darling wife, Lisa, who next to the Lord is the closest one in my life. You have shown me integrity, wisdom, love and faithfulness. I will forever be grateful to the Lord for you.

My four sons, Addison, Austin, Alexander and Arden, who continually remind me of God's goodness. You are each a treasured gift of God to me.

Our board members, for your godly counsel and wisdom.

Our staff, for your faithful support and help. Lisa and I love each of you.

Al Brice, who has pastored and spoken godly wisdom into our family and ministry.

Stephen and Joy Strang, who believed in the messages God has given Lisa and me and published them.

The entire Charisma House staff. You guys are great and fun to work with.

My many pastor and personal friends who have encouraged Lisa and me to press on to the high call.

Most of all I am eternally grateful to my Lord Jesus Christ, who has redeemed us with His own blood. You are truly wonderful.

CONTENTS

INTRODUCTION

HERE IS A door to our souls, a passage where our enemy can gain access. The presence of this portal goes undetected by many, but it is known widely in the realm of the spirit. This door stands ajar between light and darkness, with a history as ancient as the sons of Adam.

Under the divine law of God, our enemy is restricted to the realm of darkness. As believers, we are delivered from these powers of darkness. But if this door is opened, Satan and his cohorts are granted legal entrance. Their objective: to control areas of our lives. This always results in theft, destruction, and a loss of freedom. It can even mean our lives.

Jesus called these doors "gates." His exact words were "the gates of hell" (Matt. 16:18). He also said He had won the keys that locked them tight (Rev. 1:18)! But how can we shut this gate to our lives, let alone lock it—especially if we are unaware of its existence?

As a wise soldier, consider for a moment how your adversary thinks. Suppose you were an evil adversary with unrestricted and undetected access to a building. You come and go at will, slipping in to steal at whim. You enjoy your arrangement, so what do you do to insure your position and access to this building? How do you maintain your advantage? You go to great lengths to make certain the owner never detects your activity, for once your presence is discovered you are locked out.

This is exactly Satan's plan! If he can keep you ignorant, he retains his access. God says:

> My people have gone into captivity, because they have no knowledge.
>
> —ISAIAH 5:13

Ignorance comes with a high price. But we don't have to remain ignorant. This book sheds light on this deception, exposing it so you can shut and lock the devil's door permanently.

This is the third book in a series God has led me to write that exposes the traps our enemy lays. The first is *The Bait of Satan,* which shows how the enemy captures believers by the trap of offense. Though a person may have done nothing to deserve the wrong done to him, he still becomes captive if he does not forgive his offender.

The second book, *Breaking Intimidation,* shows how the fear of man paralyzes believers, causing the gift of God in their lives to become dormant due to the controlling power of intimidation.

This book, *Enemy Access Denied,* exposes the root of all the enemy's avenues of control in a believer's life. I cannot overemphasize the importance of this message. I believe it should be read by all who call on the name of Jesus. I do not say this because I wrote this book but because of the truth of God's Word in it. I am quick to admit that the wisdom this book contains is not my own. As I wrote I was acutely aware of God's hand upon me. At times my heart literally burned as I wrote. I was increasingly aware of the awesomeness of God. Under this revelation my love for Him increased. It is my prayer the same would happen as you read.

This book is not limited to enlightening you by way of instruction. It also imparts a warning. You may not shout and dance as you read some sections, yet their wisdom may spare you later agony. The concepts build on each other, so it is crucial you read this book in the order it was written. The first four chapters lay a solid and important foundation while the latter ones build upon it. You will lose the impact of one without the other.

At this point I would like to join you in prayer before you read:

> *Father, in the name of Jesus, I acknowledge my dependence on Your Holy Spirit in order to understand Your ways and Word. I ask You to reveal Your heart and will to me as I read. Give me ears to hear, eyes to see, and a heart to perceive and understand what the Spirit of God is saying. Let me not only hear, but also may my life be transformed by the work of Your Spirit. And as I close the final page, may I be able to truly say I will never be the same. I give You all the praise, glory, honor, and thanksgiving for what I am about to receive, Amen!*

May the grace of God our Father and our Lord Jesus Christ be with you.

1

THE DEVIL'S DOOR

IN THE REALM OF OVERSIGHT AND IGNORANCE, EVEN BELIEVERS FALL PREY.

MAGINE YOURSELF IN a neighborhood deluged with violence and crime. Not a day passes without some chilling news of murder, rape, or abduction. Your home is being stalked by a dangerous assailant who lurks somewhere in the dark awaiting the moment when he can slip in and take you by surprise. He longs to take you and your loved ones hostage, plunder and destroy your possessions, and maim those you love. Perhaps he'll even kill. You cannot change his mind by begging, pleading, or crying. He is a sworn enemy and determined to destroy you.

In light of all this, would you forget to lock your front door? Of course not!

Let's take it further. Would you dream of retiring at night with your front door not only unlocked but also left wide open? Absolutely not! The absurdity of it is almost offensive, yet countless people do this very thing. But it is not the door to a home that is left open—it is the door to their souls.

I have witnessed this firsthand. I have recognized them sitting in the churches where I've spoken. The location of these churches did not seem to matter. I've seen these unaware and unprepared believers from all walks of life, income, and culture. They are both overseas and stateside. They are the educated and the ignorant. But they all have one thing in common: They are victims of a wise and cunning adversary who has placed them under his controlling curse. How? They left open *the devil's door*!

This book is not about witches and spells. Nor is it about the occult practices of astrology, palm reading, or Ouija boards. All these are blatant, overt invitations to the demonic realm. Most believers would never openly dabble in these. No, I speak of something much more subtle. It operates in the realm of oversight and ignorance. In this foggy arena, even believers fall prey.

This is not a new phenomenon or unique to our generation. It is as ancient as the devil himself. It is the iniquity that caused the fall of the Morning Star, Lucifer, and displaced a third of the angels from heaven. It is rebellion, which is disobedience to God's authority.

At this point you may have breathed a sigh of relief, "Whew! This doesn't concern me. I'm not rebellious or disobedient." Not so fast! You'd be surprised. Satan is not a fool. He and his cohorts are very cunning and crafty. Most believers do not dive willfully into disobedience; rather, they fall into it by way of deception.

I'm certain you wish to know of this deception and that you desire to protect and safeguard your home, life, and family. This book is penned as a warning to protect. It contains truths that expose deception and could save your life.

DAYS OF DECEPTION

Satan is the master of deception. Jesus said he was not only a deceiver but also the very father of it (John 8:44). Jesus also warned us that his delusions and deceptions would become so strong in the latter days that if it were possible even the elect would fall prey to them (Matt. 24:24). We now live in those days. Examine Paul's passionate plea to the Corinthian church:

> For I am jealous for you with godly jealousy. For I have betrothed you to one husband, that I may present you as a chaste virgin to Christ. But I fear, lest somehow, as the serpent deceived Eve by his craftiness, so your minds may be corrupted from the simplicity that is in Christ.
>
> —2 CORINTHIANS 11:2–3

Paul compared a believer's vulnerability to deception with the deception of Eve. Eve was beguiled into disobedience. (See Genesis 3:13.) But it was a different story with Adam. "Adam was not deceived" (1 Tim. 2:14). Referring to the nature of Adam's transgression, the Scriptures say, "For just as through the *disobedience* of the one man the many were made sinners" (Rom. 5:19, NIV, emphasis added). Eve was beguiled into disobedience, but Adam knew exactly what he was doing.

I have watched some people in the church transgress God's commands with their eyes wide open, fully aware of what they are doing. They are not deceived—they are committing spiritual suicide. These people are difficult to reach.

But the majority of the disobedient, like Eve, are deceived through ignorance. My cry is for these oppressed ones. Through knowledge of the truth, the enemy can be shut off.

TWISTING GOD'S WORD

So let's look at how Satan could deceive Eve. Eve did not seem like a person who should have been susceptible to deceit. She lived in an entirely perfect environment. She had never been abused by an authority. There was no bad experience with a father, boss, or minister. She lived in a flourishing garden free of demonic influence or oppression. She'd known only God's goodness and provision as she walked and talked in His presence. So how was the serpent able to deceive her?

God commanded, "Of every tree of the garden you may freely eat; but of the tree of the knowledge of good and evil you shall not eat, for in the day that you eat of it you shall surely die" (Gen. 2:16–17).

God's goodness provided, "You may freely eat," while His authority restrained, "except the tree of the knowledge of good and evil." God emphasized their liberty to eat of every tree with the exception of one.

It is God's very essence to love and give. He desired companions in His garden who would love and obey Him. He did not want robots without the freedom of choice. He longed for children made in His image with a free will. When He restricted their access to the tree He provided a choice that protected them from death. It involved their will: Would they trust and obey? Without a command there is no choice.

Now let's examine the serpent's words. "Has God indeed said, 'You shall not eat of every tree of the garden?'" (Gen. 3:1).

The serpent ignored God's generosity and emphasized the exception, thus implying that something was being withheld from Eve. With a single question he distorted God's protective command into an unjust denial of good. Can you hear the sneer in his voice as he questioned, "So, God said you can't eat from every tree?" He made God out to be a *taker,* not the *giver* He is.

Satan led Eve down a path of reasoning where she would eventually question God's goodness and integrity. Once he accomplished this, it was a small step to turn her against God's authority.

AN ATTACK ON GOD'S AUTHORITY

Satan is sly; he was after the very foundation of God's authority. By causing the Lord to appear unjust, the serpent could attack God's dominion in Eve's mind. "Righteousness and justice are *the foundation* of His throne" (Ps. 97:2, emphasis added).

Though the woman corrected the serpent, the seed of doubt in God's goodness had been sown in her. "We may eat the fruit of the trees of the garden; but of the fruit of the tree which is in the midst of the garden, God has said, 'You shall not eat it, nor shall you touch it, lest you die'" (Gen. 3:2–3).

Even as she answered, it is quite possible that she wondered about the goodness of God. *I'm not sure why we can't eat from that tree. How could it harm us? What's in it that is so bad for us?* With these newly raised doubts, she was open to questioning God's authority.

The serpent seized this opportunity to attack God's authority, truthfulness, and integrity by boldly contradicting Him. "You will not surely die. For God knows that in the day you eat of it your eyes will be opened, and you will be like God, knowing good and evil" (Gen. 3:4–5).

The master of deception undermined the foundation of Eve's loyalty to God and assured her she would not die. Then he quickly followed his contradiction with this reasoning: "Instead of dying you'll become more like God. You'll be wise and able to choose for yourself between good and evil. Therefore you will no longer be subject to Him or His unfair commands."

REASONING THAT QUESTIONS SUBMISSION

Eve was shocked! She now wondered, *Is this why God kept this fruit from me?* She looked at the tree again but this time in a different light. She gazed at what was withheld from her. She judged the fruit

7

to be good and pleasant, not bad and injurious. She reasoned, *Surely it is desirable and will make us wise. Why should I deny myself fruit that is so good for us?*

This reasoning blinded her to all else around her. She forgot the abundant goodness and focused on the lone tree. She thought, *God has kept this from us. It could have been ours all along. Why has He done this? What else has He withheld from us?*

With the foundation of God's character, integrity, and goodness in question, there remained no reason to submit to His authority. Self-will or rebellion was the next step. Eve plucked the fruit, ate it, and gave some to her husband.

Immediately their eyes were opened. They were naked. Their disobedience brought spiritual death. By usurping God's word and submitting to Satan, they opened the devil's door, and he became their new master. They granted him not only access to their lives but also entrance into the world. Paul explained it this way: "Therefore, just as through one man sin entered the world, and death through sin, and thus death spread to all men" (Rom. 5:12).

This act of disobedience conceived destruction, sin, and sickness—a list that has multiplied and grown more foul with each passing generation. Their rebellion opened wide the door to Satan's dominion and destruction. He took full advantage of his opportunity to be like God but not subject to Him. By enslaving God's creation, he enthroned himself.

TODAY IS NO DIFFERENT

Satan's mode of operation differs little today. He still desires to pervert God's character in order to turn us against His authority.

> Do not be deceived, my beloved brethren. Every good gift and every perfect gift is from above, and comes down from the Father of lights, with whom there is no variation or shadow of turning.
> —JAMES 1:16–17

It must be settled in your heart that there is nothing good outside the realm of God's will. James shows that you can be deceived if you believe there is good outside of God's provision. Consider carefully our discussion. No matter how good it looks, tastes, or feels...no matter how rich, abundant, wise, or successful it will make you...if it is not from God, it will eventually lead to intense sorrow and end in death. Each and every perfect and good gift is from God. There is no other source. Embrace this truth and settle it in your heart. Don't let looks deceive you! If Eve had followed this admonition she never would have been swayed. But instead, she looked beyond the realm of God's provision to fulfill her desires.

How many people today marry the wrong person for the wrong reasons? God may have warned them through their parents or pastor, or showed them in their own hearts that they were making a wrong choice. But their own reasoning soon drowned out these other voices because the person they desired seemed good for companionship, pleasant to their eyes, and appeared to be wise in helping them make decisions. Ultimately they chose their will over God's. Later they suffer greatly for their misjudgment.

Many people disobey the will of God because they are enticed by the good and pleasant. Perhaps it is a means of prosperity or success outside the counsel of God's Word. They pursue their own desires and find fun, happiness, or excitement for a season. They find good in what God had said no to. They think God withholds all the attractive or fun stuff from them! They think He doesn't understand their needs and ignores the importance of their desires. They believe God is unfaithful because He doesn't answer their prayers when they expect Him to answer them. Reasoning questions, *Why wait for God's answer? Take the good and pleasant now!*

TWO SIMILAR SITUATIONS, TWO DIFFERENT RESPONSES

Consider Jesus. He was in the desert for forty days and nights. He had gone without water, food, and comfort. Hunger returned

9

because His body was close to starvation. If He didn't have food and water soon He'd die. But which came first—the provision or the temptation?

At this point Satan came to tempt Him, "If You are the Son of God, command that these stones become bread" (Matt. 4:3). Just as with Eve, Satan questioned what God had said forty days earlier when He openly declared Jesus to be His Son at the banks of the Jordan.

Satan attempted to distort God's character. "Why has He led You out here to starve? Why doesn't He provide for You? Perhaps it is time You begin to provide for Yourself. If You don't get nutrition soon You'll die or end up with severe permanent physical problems. Use Your authority to serve Yourself. Turn this stone to bread."

The children of Israel faced this same dilemma after they left Egypt and followed God into the wilderness: they ran out of food. After a mere three days, they thought God had abandoned them to die. So they began to complain. They reasoned it was better for them to have died as slaves under the oppression of the Egyptians. At least they had food there (Exod. 16). They thought God had tricked them by leading them out into the wilderness to starve. In their eyes, God was holding out on them. How deceived they were!

Their verbal complaints were the outward manifestation of their lawless hearts within. They were willing to submit to Pharaoh rather than to God's authority. They would obey whoever made it best for them. They doubted God's character. They did not want to follow God's leading because it required trusting Him. They were easily deceived into not submitting to His authority. This attitude would later cost them the Promised Land. It led them into rebellion.

Unlike the Israelites, Jesus denied Himself and waited for God's provision. He would not allow the enemy to pervert the character of God in His mind. He knew His Father would provide for His needs. He would stay submitted to God's authority no matter how unpleasant it was for the moment. He resisted Satan's temptation to take matters into His own hands; then "the devil left Him, and behold, angels came and ministered to Him" (Matt. 4:11). Why?

Who, in the days of His flesh, when He had offered up prayers and supplications, with vehement cries and tears to Him who was able to save Him from death, and was heard because of His godly fear, though He was a Son, yet He learned obedience by the things which He suffered.

—HEBREWS 5:7–8

God heard Him because of His godly fear. He did not doubt God's goodness. In the face of great temptation and intense suffering, more so than any other had undergone, He chose to obey even though it meant suffering. This kind of obedience and submission blocked all inroads of the enemy to His life. Satan had no access or entrance. The devil's door remained shut. Jesus lived in perfect obedience to His Father; therefore, He could testify on the eve of His death:

The ruler of this world is coming, and he has nothing in Me. But that the world may know that I love the Father, and as the Father gave Me commandment, so I do.

—JOHN 14:30–31

Jesus spoke of obedience when He declared that the ruler of this world, Satan, had found nothing in Him. Through perfect obedience to His Father, the door was kept securely shut against Satan. Jesus was found blameless!

TWO IMPORTANT UNIVERSAL PRINCIPLES

We have established two very important universal principles.

1. Obedience keeps the devil's door shut, denying him legal access.

2. Disobedience throws the door wide open, giving him legal access.

These principles are easy to agree with but quite difficult to live out, especially in today's culture where lawlessness abounds.

The message of this book is extremely important to every believer. It contains God's wisdom about how to avoid deception. It shows what happens once this door is open and gives insight to know if the enemy has gained entrance. It tells you how to shut the door and keep it shut! We will also see the great benefits of living in obedience, which is God's plan to help us walk in great faith and kingdom authority.

2

SACRIFICE THAT
ENSNARES

Disobedience Communicates to Those Around Us that We Know More than God Knows.

DISOBEDIENCE AND DECEPTION go hand in hand. In fact, they will increase together. We see this in an incident from the life of Saul. The prophet Samuel came to King Saul with a command from the mouth of God. "Now go and attack Amalek, and utterly destroy all that they have, and do not spare them. But kill both man and woman, infant and nursing child, ox and sheep, camel and donkey" (1 Sam. 15:3).

The command was very direct and specific. Nothing that Amalek possessed, whether human or beast, was to be left alive. With the appearance of being obedient, Saul gathered his army and went on the mission. They attacked and killed every man, woman, infant, and nursing child. Thousands were slain by Saul and his army.

However, Saul and the people spared King Agag of Amalek and the best of the sheep, oxen, fatlings, lambs, and all else that was good. Contrary to what God specifically commanded, Saul and the people who were with him probably reasoned, "It's a waste to destroy all this good livestock" (1 Sam. 15:9, 24).

Before Saul had even returned from the battle, God told Samuel Saul had disobeyed. God said He regretted that He had made Saul king. All the thousands Saul did destroy, whether people or sheep, could not make up for the few he had spared.

I HAVE OBEYED!

The next morning Saul greeted Samuel with, "Blessed are you of the LORD! I have performed the commandment of the LORD" (1 Sam. 15:13).

Saul believed he had kept the commandment of the Lord. Yet, as we'll see later, it is obvious God had a different opinion. Saul's reasoning had deceived him. This is often the case when we do not obey what God has told us. The New Testament explains:

> But be doers of the word, and not hearers only, deceiving yourselves.
>
> —JAMES 1:22

A deceived person believes he has done what is right or best when actually he is in rebellion. This is especially true of those who repeatedly disobey the Word of God. Their hearts continue to be darkened by reasoning and their deception grows greater.

Paul warned Timothy that those in the church who have not obeyed would "grow worse and worse, deceiving and being deceived" (2 Tim. 3:13). Disobedience is accompanied by deception, and both grow worse if they are not confronted. Not only do the disobedient deceive others, but they deceive themselves as well. The deception: They see themselves as right while in reality they are not.

Saul's incident with the livestock was not the first time he had practiced selective obedience. He had been rebuked previously by Samuel for not obeying. He was following a pattern of disobedience. Once this pattern forms it becomes increasingly more difficult to discern truth from error. The magnitude of disobedience grows proportionally as well. But a truly repentant heart will bring deliverance and open the eyes to the deception.

God always offers a chance for repentance. Samuel directly confronted Saul with the evidence of his disobedience: "What then is this bleating of the sheep in my ears, and the lowing of the oxen which I hear?" (1 Sam. 15:14).

Saul quickly responded, "They have brought them from the Amalekites; for the people spared the best of the sheep and the oxen, to sacrifice to the LORD your God; and the rest we have utterly destroyed" (1 Sam. 15:15).

Rather than admit his mistake, Saul shifted the blame from himself to the people. "I wanted to obey," he implied, "but the people compelled me." He had used peer pressure as an excuse for disobeying God's directives (1 Sam. 15:24). An unrepentant heart will divert the blame to others when it is caught in disobedience. It does not take responsibility for its actions.

Saul led the people; they did not lead him. He was not only accountable for his disobedience but for theirs also. He was the one with the authority to lead and the instructions on how to do it. Listen carefully, leaders, because you will give account for the disobedience you allow in those entrusted to your care.

Eli, the priest who led Israel for forty years, knew his sons were despising the ordinances of God's temple, yet he did nothing. He gave them a slap-on-the-hand rebuke, but he did not exercise his authority to remove or restrain them. Therefore God decreed, "For I have told him that I will judge his house forever for the iniquity which he knows, because his sons made themselves vile, and he did not restrain them" (1 Sam. 3:13). It was not just his sons, but Eli was judged as well.

GREATER EFFORT DOES NOT INDICATE OBEDIENCE

So, first Saul blamed the people. Then he pointed out that they spared the animals for a good cause—to sacrifice them as offerings before the Lord. You know Saul is deceived if he thinks that through disobedience he can offer a sacrifice or service to God that would be acceptable.

This is a most deceptive form of rebellion. We see it in the life of Cain, the firstborn son of Adam, who also brought a sacrifice that the Lord would not accept. He brought the fruit of his field as an offering to the Lord. We know it was brought forth with much toil because God had earlier cursed the ground (Gen. 3:17–19). Cain had to clear the ground of rocks, stumps, and other debris. Then he plowed and cultivated the soil. He planted, watered, fertilized, and protected his crops. He had put much effort in his service toward God. But it was a sacrifice of his own making, not the one prescribed by God. It represented his service to God in his own strength and ability rather than by obedience.

Abel, Adam's second son, brought the choice firstborn of his flock and their fat and offered them to the Lord. We know he also had to work hard while tending his flocks, but it's unlikely that he worked as hard as Cain.

Working hard does not necessarily mean you are doing what is right. The longer I walk with the Lord, the more I discover that sometimes the busier I am, the less I accomplish. Busyness does not equate to obedience.

When the offerings were presented, "the LORD respected Abel and his offering, but He did not respect Cain and his offering. And Cain was very angry and his countenance fell" (Gen. 4:4–5).

Both brothers knew God's requirements because they had learned of God's ways from their parents. They had heard how their mother and father had attempted to cover their nakedness with fig leaves. These leaves represented their own attempt to cover their sin. God then demonstrated His acceptable offering by slaying an innocent animal and covering Adam and Eve with its skin. So Adam and Eve knew that animal sacrifice was the acceptable way to cover sin.

God told Cain that he knew the "right" thing to do (Gen. 4:7). Yet Cain had tried to win God's acceptance apart from His counsel. God responded by showing what He would accept. His desire is for man's obedience, not his sacrificial acts.

SIN LIES AT THE DOOR

God confronted Cain's sin and gave him a chance to repent.

> Why are you angry? And why has your countenance fallen? If you do well, will you not be accepted? And if you do not do well, *sin lies at the door.* And its desire is for you, but you should rule over it.
>
> —GENESIS 4:6–7, EMPHASIS ADDED

Cain had to choose. The devil was at the door. Would Cain rebel against God's command and invite Satan in? Or would he choose to rule over sin and deny Satan access?

How could Cain rule over sin? The same way Jesus did: by living in obedience to God the Father. Recall Jesus' words, "The ruler of this world is coming, and he has nothing in me" (John 14:30). Sin and the devil had nothing in Jesus because of His perfect obedience to the Father. Sin could crouch at the door all it wanted. Jesus' door was shut!

But Cain did not master sin. He allowed offense, betrayal, and hatred to enter the door to his life. Cain rose up and slew his brother in rage. Cain started out attempting to serve God. He was even fervent in his effort. But disobedience, lack of repentance, and offense gave way to murder.

We see some of the cruelest things done by those who, like Cain

19

and Saul, serve the Lord their own way. They may even begin with good motives, but their independent hearts soon manifest in difficult times. Many innocent ones (like Abel) are wounded or killed by these religious crusaders, those who are carrying out their own will in the name of the Lord.

THE UNSPOKEN MESSAGE

When Samuel confronted Saul with his deception, Samuel reminded him of a few things. Before he made any more excuses, Samuel silenced Saul by saying:

> "Be quiet! And I will tell you what the LORD said to me last night." And he [Saul] said to him, "Speak on." So Samuel said, "When you were little in your own eyes, were you not head of the tribes of Israel? And did not the LORD anoint you king over Israel? Now the LORD sent you on a mission, and said, 'Go, and utterly destroy the sinners, the Amalekites, and fight against them until they are consumed.' Why then did you not obey the voice of the LORD? Why did you swoop down on the spoil, and do evil in the sight of the LORD?"
>
> —1 SAMUEL 15:16–19

At one time Saul had been unassuming, humble, and meek. In fact, when Samuel first told Saul that he would rule Israel, Saul responded, "Am I not a Benjamite, of the smallest of the tribes of Israel, and my family the least of all the families of the tribe of Benjamin? Why then do you speak like this to me?" (1 Sam. 9:21). Saul actually hid on the day Samuel was to announce who would be king (1 Sam. 10:21–22).

He had been small in his own eyes. Samuel brought this to his remembrance, then proceeded, "Now the LORD sent you on a mission, and said, 'Go, and utterly destroy'...Why did you swoop down on the spoil and do evil in the sight of the LORD?"

In other words Samuel asked, "Saul, when did your wisdom begin to override God's? What happened to your humble, unassuming spirit? Why do you now think you know more than the Lord?"

Do you think you know more than God? Of course not! But when we are disobedient, that is exactly the message we communicate to God and those around us. How foolish to think we could ever be wiser than the One who sits on the throne of glory, the very One who not only created the universe but also contains the universe, the Creator who put the stars in the heavens with His fingers. Yet we exalt our wisdom above His when we ignore His counsel!

When Moses led the children of Israel through the wilderness, God showed His mighty power through him. After years of wandering they came to a place called Kadesh where the people complained about the lack of water. This wasn't the first time they had run out of water. Earlier, at Rephidim, God instructed Moses to strike a certain rock and water would come forth, which it did (Exod. 17:6).

This time the Lord instructed Moses, "Speak to the rock before their [the congregation's] eyes, and it will yield its water" (Num. 20:8). Moses gathered the congregation together. But instead of speaking to the rock as God commanded, he did what he had previously done. He struck the rock and did it twice.

Moses disobeyed God's word. Amazingly water still came out in abundance. Even though Moses disobeyed, God still provided water for His people. It would appear that God had blessed Moses' disobedience.

But later God spoke to Moses, "Because you did not trust in me enough to honor me as holy in the sight of the Israelites, you will not bring this community into the land I give them" (Num. 20:12, NIV).

You can't ignore what God is telling you to do now because of what He told you earlier. This one act of disobedience cost Moses entrance to the Promised Land. Why did hitting a rock cost him so dearly? Because Moses honored his wisdom above the directive of God. He did it his way, not God's way.

He acted as if he knew better than God how to obtain water from the rock. He had subjected God's word to the approval of a mere man! This explains why God said, "You did not honor Me!"

Disobedience communicates to God and those around us that we think we know more than God. Thus we dishonor Him. This tears down His authority in our lives.

No sane person would go against God's direct command. That is why deceit is such an element of disobedience, even if we're only deceiving ourselves. Human reasoning must never override divine direction.

PAYING THE PRICE

Moses and Saul were both leaders. The price of their disobedience was great. The more mature we are, the greater our judgment for disobedience. James 3:1 says, "My brethren, let not many of you become teachers, knowing that we shall receive a stricter judgment." My four-year-old son can do childish, immature things and receive only a minor correction. However, if my ten-year-old son did the same thing it would merit greater discipline.

Hear the word of the Lord, those of you in leadership. Your responsibility and accountability are much greater. Be a strong leader in obedience to God. Do not allow your strength to lie in the approval and acceptance of those you lead. Nor let your strength tempt you to harshness or intimidation over people. The greatest leaders in the kingdom are those who obey God, even when great pressure is on them. God's Word and His way will always prove perfect in the end.

3

OBEDIENCE— NOT SACRIFICE

IF WE DO NOT LAY DOWN OUR LIVES, WE WILL FIND A WAY OF FULFILLING OUR OWN WILLS.

AFTER I HAD been a Christian approximately seven years, I served on the staff for a church that stressed the importance of exercising faith to receive God's blessings. By contrast, in my personal life I was crying out with a deep desire to know God for who He was as opposed to what He could do for me. God began to introduce me to holiness and the crucified life, concepts that were nearly foreign to me.

Back then I was an avid fan of the Dallas Cowboys. Every Sunday during football season I came home from church and turned on the game. I waited to change out of my suit during a commercial. If my wife needed help, forget it. "Honey, the Cowboys are playing!" We ate lunch at halftime or after the game.

On one particular Sunday there was a crucial game. The Dallas Cowboys were playing the Philadelphia Eagles. The winner would earn a seat in the playoffs; the loser would be eliminated.

The game was exciting, with only eight minutes left. The Cowboys were behind by four points, but they had the ball and were on the move. I kept thinking, *They're going to drive the ball down the field and win this game in the last few minutes like they've done many times before.* I was on my feet in my living room along with the crowd in the stadium.

All of a sudden the Spirit of God entreated me to pray! The burden was tremendous. I knew it wasn't something to which I could respond later. It was for now!

I pleaded, "Lord, there are only eight minutes left in the game. Wait and I'll pray five hours when this game is over."

How could eight minutes hurt anything? I reasoned. *Surely I can pray about whatever He wants me to after this game.* But the urgency and burden did not lift; it became stronger.

I bargained again, "Lord, I'll pray the rest of the day and even into the evening if I have to. Just let me watch these last couple of minutes."

After all, I thought, *I'm being generous!* But the burden remained, and there was a deep knowing within that my negotiations had been denied.

I comforted myself with what I thought was a fair compromise. *I'll pray for hours. Surely nothing could happen in the next few minutes that couldn't be covered in five hours of prayer.* I knew it was a compromise I could keep because the rest of my day was free.

So, do you know what I did? I watched the rest of the game. When it was over I immediately marched off to my bedroom and locked the door behind me. I got down on my face, prepared to pray for a minimum of five hours. I meant what I had promised.

For fifteen minutes I wrestled and tried to pray, but it was a struggle. It was as dry and boring as any prayer could be. The urgency and ability to pray was gone. The burden had lifted. I knew I had been wrong. Conviction overwhelmed me. God showed me that what I wanted had taken greater importance than what He desired. After several minutes of dry silence, God spoke, "Son, I don't want your five hours of sacrifice. I want obedience!"

These words riveted me. I lay speechless before a holy God. How could I have been so deceived as to count the eight minutes trivial when God was calling me then. How could I have treated His desire and will so lightly! I had chosen a carnal football game over obeying God.

THE CROSS SYMBOLIZES OBEDIENCE

Jesus made this statement, "If anyone desires to come after Me, let him deny himself, and take up his cross, and follow Me" (Matt. 16:24).

Some take up the cross and concentrate on its image of suffering, which represents a life of sacrifice. However, in this verse the cross is not the end result. It enables us to obey. You can live a life of self-denial and sacrifice yet not "follow Him." In fact, you could choose self-denial and sacrifice and still be in rebellion against God!

The focus of what Jesus is saying is *obedience!* The only way we can obey is to take up the cross. For without death to our own agendas and desires we will eventually have a face-off between the will of God and the desire of man. If we do not lay down our lives we will find a way of fulfilling our own wills and even use scriptures to back it!

Sacrifice was scriptural, so Saul was *scriptural* in his desire to sacrifice animals as offerings. But he was *disobedient* to God's directive. Does service to God include disobedience? If so, Satan would receive glory from our "scriptural" religious practices or sacrifices. He is the originator of rebellion. But God declares, "Has the LORD as great delight in burnt offerings and sacrifices as in obeying the voice of the LORD? Behold, to obey is better than sacrifice" (1 Sam. 15:22).

For the rest of the chapter I want to unwrap this concept, using Isaiah as a guide.

I AM GOD—THERE IS NO ONE LIKE ME

Have you ever gone on a job interview? You put on your best clothing, labor over your hair, and carry a roll of breath mints. Why? Because of the status of the person you're about to meet. Before Isaiah discusses obedience and sacrifice, he gives us a glimpse of the One we're being asked to obey.

> Thus says the LORD:
> "Heaven is My throne,
> And earth is My footstool.
> Where is the house that you will build Me?
> And where is the place of My rest?
> For all those things My hand has made,
> And all those things exist,"
> Says the LORD.
>
> —ISAIAH 66:1–2

Let's translate to our modern-day terminology. God said, "I live in heaven; it is My throne. I made the earth; it's a footstool before My throne. I am bigger than you are even capable of thinking. I am God."

Stop and meditate on this. Perhaps you will catch a glimpse of His awesome glory! He created the earth and the universe. He positioned the stars with His fingers! Most of us do not comprehend the vastness of the universe. Because I have a background in engineering, I've researched some of the fascinating facts we know about the vastness of God's creation.

Light travels at the speed of 186,000 miles per second (not per hour but per second). That is roughly 700 million miles per hour. Our modern airplanes fly approximately 500 miles per hour.

The moon is roughly 239,000 miles from the earth. If we were to travel to the moon by plane, it would take us twenty days. But light travels there in 1.3 seconds!

Let's continue. The sun is 93 million miles from the earth. To reach the sun by plane, your journey would last over twenty-one years. Think of how long the past twenty-one years of your life has been. Then imagine flying that long without stopping to reach the sun! For those of you who prefer driving, it would take you roughly two hundred years, without any rest stops! Yet it takes light only eight minutes and twenty seconds to travel from the sun to the earth!

The nearest star is 4.5 light-years from the earth. To reach it by plane would take approximately fifty-three billion years! That is 53 with nine zeros behind it! Yet light reaches it in only four and one-half years!

The average star you can see unassisted with the naked eye is 100 to 1,000 light-years away. I wouldn't even attempt to calculate the amount of time it would take for a plane to reach it. But think of it: Light traveling at a rate of 186,000 miles per second takes one thousand years to reach the earth. That means there are stars you see at night whose light emanated from them in the days of King Richard's reign in England, and it has been traveling at the rate of 700 million miles per hour ever since, without slowing down! That light originated seven hundred years before America became a nation!

Let's expand this further. In the mid-nineties NASA's Hubble Space Telescope sent back pictures of galaxies that were 7,000 light-years away! Our minds cannot even comprehend distances like these. Are you getting a greater glimpse of His glory?

"WHAT DO YOU THINK YOU CAN DO FOR ME?"

God put these stars in place with His fingers. The entire universe cannot contain Him (1 Kin. 8:27). Isaiah 40:12 tells us that God measured all the waters of the earth in the palm of His hand and measured the universe with the breadth of His hand (NIV). What glory!

From this context look at the question God asked through Isaiah.

He said, "Heaven is My throne, and earth is My footstool. Where is the house that you will build Me?" God was saying, "I am God; consider My glory, My ability, My power. What can you add to what I do?" Another way to say it is, "What do you think you can do for Me?" Do you get His point?

I am reminded of the words of Solomon at the close of his full and prosperous life.

> I know that whatever God does,
> It shall be forever.
> Nothing can be added to it,
> And nothing taken from it.
> God does it, that men should fear before Him.
>
> —ECCLESIASTES 3:14

There's a big difference between the works that we do and the works that God does. When God does it, *nothing* can be added, and *nothing* can be subtracted. In contrast, Psalm 127:1 says, "Unless the LORD builds the house, they labor in vain who build it." Notice you *can* labor in service for God on your own, but it will be vain or of no eternal value.

Nothing changes or takes away from God's plans. Even if we labor in vain or set ourselves against His purposes, His intentions will be fulfilled.

Joseph's ten older brothers assumed that when they sold Joseph into slavery, they aborted God's plan to make Joseph a ruler. However, their evil scheme actually brought forth the fulfillment of God's plan. (See Genesis 37–45.)

Solomon said:

> That which is has already been,
> And what is to be has already been;
> And God requires an account of what is past.
>
> —ECCLESIASTES 3:15

The course is set already. That which is and that which is to come has already been in the mind of God. This shows His sovereignty. But God does require an account of what is past. This is to say, we will account for our obedience or disobedience to His ordained will. This illustrates the free will of man.

Some will say, "If this is the case, then man can subtract from what God does by just not doing what He planned." No, because God knows the end from the beginning. He knows what each person will do before they do it. He does not author it, for He is not the author of evil. But He does use it in His majestic wisdom. Hallelujah! Are you glimpsing His glory?

There are two ways a person can disobey. First, when you do what God has not told you to do and, second, when you do not do what you've been told to do. This is why Solomon said, "And God requires an account of what is past."

THE SON CAN DO NOTHING OF HIMSELF

Jesus did no more or less than what He saw His Father do. He did not add to or take away from it, which was in complete contrast to the religious leaders of His day. Examine closely these two quotes of Jesus, making note of the word *nothing*:

> Then Jesus answered and said to them, "Most assuredly, I say to you, the Son *can do nothing of Himself,* but what He sees the Father do; for whatever He does, the Son also does in like manner.
>
> —JOHN 5:19, EMPHASIS ADDED

> *I can of Myself do nothing.* As I hear, I judge; and My judgment is righteous, because I do not seek My own will but the will of the Father who sent Me.
>
> —JOHN 5:30, EMPHASIS ADDED

Jesus did not minister for the first thirty years of His life. Can you imagine it? He knew He was the Messiah when He was twelve. We know this because His parents found Him in the temple listening and asking questions. When they asked Him why, He responded, "Did you not know that I must be about My Father's business?" He then went home with them and was subject to them until the age of thirty (Luke 2:41–52). We further confirm this by the fact that His first miracle was at the age of thirty at the wedding of Cana (John 2:11).

Can you see Him as a twenty-five-year-old man as He passed the blind, deaf, crippled, and leprous lining the streets of Nazareth? He could have laid hands on them and healed them. But He did not. He waited. He made furniture, faithfully attended synagogue, and roamed the hills of Galilee in prayer until He was thirty. Not launching Himself or His ministry, He waited for the Father's ordination.

At the age of thirty He went to John to be baptized in order to fulfill all righteousness. It was then that His Father declared from heaven, "This is My beloved Son, in whom I am well pleased" (Matt. 3:17). Well pleased! He hadn't done anything but make furniture and walk the hills of Galilee. Yet the reason for God's pleasure was Jesus' perfect obedience in all things, even if these did not include what we would call ministry.

THE MINISTRY OF JESUS

Now look forward at His ministry. There are many incidents that reflect His perfect obedience. Let's look at a few:

There was a man, Lazarus, whom Jesus loved. He had two sisters, Martha and Mary. Lazarus became very ill to the point of death, so his sisters sent word to Jesus.

When their messengers found Jesus, they relayed the urgency and fears of Lazarus's sisters and waited for His response. "So, when He heard that he was sick, He stayed two more days in the place where He was" (John 11:6).

The messengers probably argued, "Maybe we did not make it clear, Jesus. He is so sick that he will die! You must hurry!" Yet Jesus wasn't moved.

The sun set on the first day, and all those around Him looked at each other with questions in their eyes, "Doesn't Jesus care? Why hasn't He left for Bethany? It's been hours since we told Him the news. What kind of friend is He?" Jesus sensed their questions and disappointment, yet He still didn't move.

Notice the marked difference between Jesus' lack of action and Saul's make-it-happen, make-them-happy mind-set. Saul knew God's command but succumbed to the pressure of the people. (See 1 Samuel 15:24.) He gave in and gave them what they wanted. He appeased men yet disobeyed God. How often do we disobey our Father to appease our brothers?

Jesus did only what His Father said! After two days passed, Jesus said, "Let's go to Lazarus."

The messengers may have thought, *If you knew You were going to go, why didn't You leave two days ago? Why now?* There was a reason, "The Son can do nothing of Himself, but what He sees the Father do" (John 5:19).

The Lord showed me how I would have responded if Lazarus had been my friend. I would have jumped in my car, ran into his house, and laid hands on him. All of this would be done without as much as a thought of seeking the Spirit of God for His direction.

I had the church mentality of "wherever I go, God goes—and He will do whatever I ask Him while I'm there." Yes, He will never leave you or forsake you, but to view God as subject to our will is backward thinking. We do not lead while God follows. No, God leads, and we follow—if we are wise (John 12:26). As we follow, He instructs us.

We have mistakenly thought that if we laid hands on the sick, independent of the Spirit's leading, God was obligated to heal and confirm our lead by following with His signs. If this were true, we should go empty the hospitals. We get discouraged when God does not follow our lead with His healing and miracles. God will heal and perform miracles, but it is as He leads and we follow.

There are many references in the Gospels of, "He healed them all." But they were not universal occurrences. Take, for instance, all the sick, blind, lame, and paralyzed people Jesus left at the pool of Bethesda after He healed the man with the infirmity of thirty-eight years (John 5). Why did He walk in and heal the one and not touch the rest?*

How about the man, lame from his mother's womb, who was laid daily at the gate of the temple? Jesus passed him each time He entered the temple. Why didn't Jesus heal him? Because His Father hadn't instructed Him to do so. Yet it was God's will for this man to be healed. Later Peter and John raised him up under the direction of the Holy Spirit (Acts 3).

Neither did Jesus minister by formulas. He spit on one, laid hands on some, and simply spoke to others. He formed balls of mud and placed them in eye sockets and sent others to the priests. Why the variety? Because He wasn't following a formula—He was doing what He saw His Father do!

I WILL PAY ATTENTION TO THIS ONE

This is how God wants His children to serve Him. He desires us to come to the place where we will only do what we see Him do. That includes doing nothing when God is silent. He longs for us to leave behind the sacrifices based on what we think, want, or are pressured to do and return to simple obedience to Him. Remember, Isaiah pointed out that all our sacrifice can't give God anything He doesn't already have.

> Thus says the LORD:
> "Heaven is My throne,
> And earth is My footstool.

---

* I am not questioning God's willingness to heal. Scripture states that God heals all diseases (Ps. 103:3). I am merely dealing with healing in the light of God's leading in our lives to minister to others.

Where is the house that you will build Me?" . . .
But on this one will I look:
On him who is poor and of a contrite spirit,
And who trembles at My word."

—Isaiah 66:1–2

When we are overwhelmed by our inadequacies, our awesome Father promises to pay attention and uphold the humble man who trembles at His word. Whew! The humblest, meekest man is the one who gets God's attention.

I have comprised a revealing list containing some of the characteristics of one who trembles at God's word. Meditate on these:

1. Obedience is immediate.

2. God's will is honored above all else.

3. There is no arguing, complaining, or pouting.

4. They search for the heartbeat of God.

5. When God's will is unclear, they wait until it is.

6. They suffer the rejection of friends rather than displease God.

7. They do not add or take away from what God says.

8. There is an awe for God's ways and wisdom, for there is none greater.

Isaiah tells us in graphic terms about God's attitude toward sacrifices that are not out of obedience.

He who kills a bull is as if he slays a man;
He who sacrifices a lamb, as if he breaks a dog's neck;
He who offers a grain offering, as if he offers swine's blood;
He who burns incense, as if he blesses an idol.

—Isaiah 66:3

Didn't God ordain the lamb and bull sacrifices? Wasn't He the One who ordained the grain offering? Wasn't it God who instructed Moses to burn incense in the holy place of the tabernacle?

So why now does He compare the sacrifice of the lamb and bull to the killing of a man or the breaking of a dog's neck? Why does He say their offerings are like an unclean pig's blood? Why does He liken the incense offered (a shadow of their worship and prayer) to the blessing of an idol?

> Just as they have chosen their own ways,
> And their soul delights in their abominations,
> So will I choose their delusions,
> And bring their fears on them;
> Because, when I called, no one answered,
> When I spoke they did not hear;
> But they did evil before My eyes,
> And chose that in which I do not delight.
>
> —ISAIAH 66:3–4

When God called, no one answered. When He spoke, no one listened! The people were so busy "serving God" with religious sacrifices (God called them "abominations") that they did not respond in obedience to His voice! God lamented their choice, "They chose sacrifice over listening and obeying My voice." He made it clear that His delight is not in sacrifice!

BUSY BUT NOT OBEDIENT

What about today? Are we so busy serving God with intercessory prayer, generous offerings, orderly services, outreaches, ministry administration, fastings, Bible studies, Christian conferences and conventions that we are missing what He is saying? Caught up in it all, have we lost the simplicity of hearing His voice and trembling at His word?

Today it is very easy to build a ministry machine yet lose the focus of its purpose. It is easy to succumb to the pressure of workloads, financial obligations, maintaining our status, the demands of controlling people, and all else that tries to dictate our course. But what about obedience to the Spirit of God?

Can we follow as He leads, or are we bound by charismatic, full gospel service order? Perhaps our services are not ordered by a written bulletin such as is the case in many denominations, but the truth is many nondenominational churches have set service orders, too—they just are not written out. So we scorn those who are honest enough to write out their order of service, judging them as "bound and not free like us."

Our order is clear. It's praise, then worship (by the way, praise is the fast songs and worship is the slow ones, in case you're not sure what the difference is), followed by announcements, offering, the message, altar call, and possibly laying hands on some people in the hope they will fall over. We boast in this freedom of worship. But in actuality we've been delivered from hymnals only to be bound to transparencies. Yet all the while we believe ourselves to be Spirit-led.

This attitude places us in a vulnerable position. We become highly susceptible to the type of disobedience found in King Saul, believing that having all components for ministry is more crucial than obedience to God. In this setting God will not compete for our attention. He stands back and watches as we carry on.

This is not limited to ministry alone. It occurs on a personal level as well. Returning to my example of the Dallas Cowboy's football game, I had been a Christian for quite awhile. I served diligently in full-time ministry, often fifty to seventy hours a week and at Sunday services. I was often the last one to leave the building. Having done all this, when the Spirit of God came upon me to pray, I felt I could ignore His calling voice because, after all, I was His faithful, hardworking servant.

So by my unspoken attitude I was asserting to God that I had the right to pick and choose when I would listen to and obey His voice. It was optional because I was so loyal and hardworking. We must remember that a thousand acts of obedience do not justify one act of disobedience!

ENEMY ACCESS DENIED

That I could have been so ignorant and arrogant now makes me want to weep. Jesus gave His very life for me, and I smugly judged His leading as optional because of my menial works! May God keep us from the subtle deception that leads to disobedience!

4

THE MYSTERY OF
LAWLESSNESS

FOR REBELLION IS
WITCHCRAFT...

THE WORD *WITCHCRAFT* conjures up images of women in black, reciting incantations, traveling by broom, and scanning the future via a crystal ball while their cauldron simmers on the fire. Or perhaps the more modern view is one who casts spells and curses upon others for influence or gain. Let's leave behind both of these concepts and discover the heart of witchcraft, no matter what form it takes.

Samuel identified witchcraft in the life of Saul when he told Saul:

Behold, to obey is better than sacrifice,
And to heed than the fat of rams.
For rebellion *is as* the sin of witchcraft,
And stubbornness *is as* iniquity and idolatry.

—1 Samuel 15:22–23

Notice Samuel directly linked rebellion with witchcraft, "For rebellion *is as* the sin of witchcraft."*

The Hebrew word used here for *witchcraft* is *qesem*. Its English counterparts are *divination, witchcraft,* and *sorcery.* However, experts say the exact usage of these words in reference to occultism is unknown. This accounts for the various translations of the word *witchcraft.*[2] The importance lies not in the label but in the result of witchcraft.

This text should read, "For rebellion *is* witchcraft." This clarifies the context of this scripture. It is one thing to liken rebellion to witchcraft, but it is an entirely different issue to say it actually is witchcraft. Obviously a true Christian would never practice witchcraft knowingly. But how many today are under its influence because of the deception of rebellion?

Witchcraft in any form has the same result: it directly opens one up to the demonic realm. Its goal is to control circumstances, situations, or people. This is accomplished through various avenues often without the participant's understanding of what is happening in the spirit realm. Consciousness ranges from total ignorance of what one is doing to a complete understanding and awareness of the powers of darkness involved. The goal of witchcraft is to control, but inevitably the controller becomes the controlled due to involvement with the demonic realm.

---

* Notice the words *is as* in this verse are italic type. This is commonly used in the New King James and King James versions for words that did not appear in the original text. They were added later by the translators to lend clarity. A more accurate translation would have used only the word *is.*[1]

REBELLION OPENS THE DOOR
TO CONTROLLING POWERS

As a former youth pastor, I came in contact with a large amount of blatant occult practices in the state of Florida. Many high school students dabble in the occult to various degrees. Youth group leaders regularly reported encounters with classmates who were involved in witchcraft.

I learned that when an individual was initiated into a coven (a group practicing witchcraft), the leaders compelled him or her to take drugs, drink, engage in illicit sex, steal, and commit various other acts that defied the laws of God and our land. I was uncertain why this was encouraged until God opened the truth to me that "rebellion is witchcraft."

By rebelling against the laws of God, their parents, and their society, the participants either knowingly or unknowingly grant legal access to the controlling demonic realm. Why? Rebellion is witchcraft. The more they rebel, the more they give legal right for demonic powers to influence and control them.

You may be wondering why I used the term *legal right*. That's because God has ordained laws of order in the spiritual realm. Under the divine law of God, the devil's authority has been restricted to the realm of darkness. Therefore, disobedience to God's authority, whether direct or delegated, moves a person out of spiritual light and into spiritual darkness where the enemy has legal access. (See 1 Thessalonians 5:5 and Matthew 6:24.)

Those who willfully commit themselves to the service of Satan understand this principle, yet others are deceived. These others are ignorant and mistake lawlessness for liberty, so they rebel claiming they are free. But there is no freedom in rebellion. The New Testament reveals a clear picture of what actually takes place. The rebellious become slaves to depravity. Peter exposed their error this way:

> They proudly boast about their sins and conquests, and, using
> lust as their bait, they lure [by saying] . . . "Do what you like, be

43

free." But these very teachers who offer this "freedom" from the law are themselves slaves to sin and destruction. For a man is a slave to whatever controls him.

—2 PETER 2:18–19, TLB

The truth is evident. There is no freedom but instead bondage and control in rebellion. It is the opening of the soul to demonic oppression and control. Paul reemphasized this point:

Don't you realize that you can choose your own master? You can choose sin (with death) or else obedience (with acquittal). The one to whom you offer yourself—he will take you and be your master and you will be his slave.

—ROMANS 6:16, TLB

RESIST THROUGH SUBMISSION

Cain had the choice to honor God's will and close the door to sin's demonic control (witchcraft), or he could honor his own will in rebellion and welcome the crouching form of sin that sought to master (control) him (Gen. 4:7).

How was Cain to close the door? The New Testament tells us:

God resists the proud, but gives grace to the humble. Therefore submit to God. Resist the devil and he will flee from you.

—JAMES 4:6–7

As we resist the devil by submitting to God, we close tight our door to the enemy. Submission is obedience. It is not limited to actions alone but also encompasses the realm of the heart.

Many try resisting the devil by quoting scriptures and praying fervently, and this is a legitimate form of spiritual warfare. However, some people do this yet remain disobedient to God's authority in other areas. When this is the case, the devil just laughs. Their disobedience has granted him legal access, and he is a legalist. They can bind and loose till they are blue in the face, but the sad fact remains that their lack of submission overrides the words they vainly speak.

Cain's downfall progressed this way: First, he harbored an offense against his brother. Hatred entered his heart, then deception, which paved the way for murder.

When sin entered Cain's life, it caused him to do what he never could have imagined doing. If, as a young man, he had been told, "One day you will murder your brother," he probably would have responded, "You're crazy. I could never do such a thing." Yet he did. Why? Disobedience had opened the door of his soul to sin, and it mastered him.

Rebellion also opened Saul's soul to the influence of a controlling spirit, which caused him to behave in a manner he never would have when he was in his right mind. The Bible indicates that it was not long after his rebellion that an evil tormenting spirit came upon his life and troubled him (1 Sam. 16:14). This evil spirit manipulated his life from that point on. There was no deliverance for Saul because there was no repentance from his sin.

Saul became a very different man from the one we first met. He had been unassuming before he was king. He obeyed his father and respected the things of God. If you had approached him then and foretold, "Saul, the day will come when you will kill eighty-five innocent priests, their wives, and their children in a fit of rage," he would have dismissed you as crazy and countered with, "I could never do that!" The sad truth is he did (1 Sam. 22:17–18). That evil spirit caused him to live a life of jealousy, anger, hatred, strife, murder, and deception. It legally controlled him by way of his unrepentant rebellion.

KEEP THE RIGHT FOCUS

Because we're discussing witchcraft, I want to warn you about a deception that happens to believers who are often trying the hardest to thwart Satan.

I knew a pastor who was into reading Christian books on combating the occult. They were all he talked about. He believed he was under intense spiritual warfare. His discussions were no longer about Jesus but centered on the evil forces he was fighting. I warned him that his focus was getting sidetracked, but he ignored my advice and assumed I was not versed in spiritual warfare.

A year went by, and he came to me, "John, do you remember the warning you gave me?"

"Yes," I nodded.

He told me, "God had me burn every one of those books. I have never lived under so much fear in all my life. Those books diverted my focus from Jesus to Satan."

The Bible says we are to keep our eyes on Jesus, the author and finisher of our faith (Heb. 12:2). Focus on Jesus! If the devil gets in the way, resist him fervently and continue your pursuit of Jesus. If we focus on evil and the occult, we are eventually ensnared by its seduction. What you focus on becomes your source of direction, and if your focus is steered off course long enough, it becomes your destination.

THE MAN OF LAWLESSNESS

In 1990, while changing channels in a hotel room, my wife and I came across a network special on satanism and witchcraft. Because I don't like to expose myself to the occult, I was about to flip the channel, but I felt impressed to watch it for a moment. The program discussed the satanic bible.

I was shocked to find out what the first commandment in this bible was: "Do what thou will."

It hit me like a ton of bricks. This is a direct perversion of the life of Jesus. He said, "I do not seek My own will but the will of the Father who sent Me" (John 5:30).

I turned off the program, knowing I had seen all I needed to see. I began to ponder. Jesus had the Spirit of God without measure.

> For since He Whom God has sent speaks the words of God
> [proclaims God's own message], God does not give Him His
> Spirit sparingly or by measure.
>
> —JOHN 3:34, AMP

From the testimony of John we discover the reason Jesus was filled with the Spirit of God without measure. He only did and only spoke the will and words of His Father. His perfected obedience gave Him complete fullness of the Spirit, for our God gives His Holy Spirit to those who obey Him! (See Acts 5:32.)

To be self-willed, doing and saying whatever you will, is rebellion, and rebellion is witchcraft. Just as Jesus was filled with the Spirit of God without measure due to His perfect obedience, perfect disobedience brings demonic influence without measure.

This is seen in the life of the Antichrist. Scriptures refer to him as the lawless one (2 Thess. 2:8). He is described as the one "who opposes and exalts himself above all that is called God or that is worshiped, so that he sits as God in the temple of God, showing himself that he is God" (2 Thess. 2:4). His is a life of perfected rebellion toward God.

This verse has two levels of meaning. Yes, he will probably sit down in the physical temple of God. But he is also practicing perfect rebellion in his own body. Scriptures call our bodies the temple of the Holy Spirit.

Why will the Antichrist have the power of Satan without measure? Because his rebellion is perfect and complete. Rebellion, remember, is witchcraft. It grants Satan legal entrance into a life. In perfect disobedience this man will carry the unchecked spirit of Satan.

> The coming of the lawless one is according to the working of Satan, with all power, signs, and lying wonders.
> —2 Thessalonians 2:9

This lawless one will be the very antithesis of our Lord and Christ. That is why he is called Antichrist.

> Little children, it is the last hour; and as you have heard that the Antichrist is coming, even now many antichrists have come, by which we know that it is the last hour.
> —1 John 2:18

Though this applies to every generation since John's day, it is a prophetic scripture that zeroes in to the final generation before the return of Christ. Peter, in writing about the last days, says, "Do not forget this one thing, that with the Lord one day is as a thousand years, and a thousand years as one day" (2 Pet. 3:8). One of God's days is equal to a thousand of our years. Divide one thousand years by twenty-four, and you have the amount of years for one of God's hours, approximately forty years. So when John says "last hour" he is referring to the final generation, which many believe is our own.

Notice the close of this scripture, "even now many antichrists have come, by which we know that it is the last hour." This man of lawlessness will not suddenly appear without warning or preparation. Before his appearance complete rebellion will seem common, since a large measure of lawlessness will already be at work in society.

The Mystery of Lawlessness at Work Today

In Paul's instructions to the Thessalonians, he talks again about the condition of lawlessness and rebellion prior to the revelation of the lawless one:

> For the mystery of lawlessness (that hidden principle of rebellion against constituted authority) is already at work in the world.
>
> —2 Thessalonians 2:7, amp

The mystery of lawlessness is the hidden principle that rebellion is witchcraft. This principle is already at work, and the lawlessness will progressively worsen until the man of lawlessness is revealed. This perfected rebellion will not come as a shock because the mystery of lawlessness has already been at work in our society and churches.

You may question, "Churches, too?" Yes, it is where the work of lawlessness is the most deceptive. In many ways the spirit of the world has crept into the church. Rebellion is increasingly becoming an acceptable way of life. There are many aspects of rebellion that we now consider normal that would have horrified not only the church but also society forty years ago (for example, how children treat parents, how people talk about their pastors, disrespect toward political leaders, the lack of ethics in business, and so on).

This same acceptance has spilled over to the church. These thought patterns are contrary to obedience but have developed in the mind of believers. We'll discuss them later in this book.

We need to change our thinking. The kingdom of God is not a democracy but a *kingdom* ruled by the *King*. It is structured by a royal order, rank, and law. Members of the kingdom are subject to them—they are not optional. They are not subject to us, but we are subject to them. There are consequences when they are overlooked, ignored, trespassed, or blatantly violated.

Jesus forewarned us of this when His disciples asked for indications of His second coming. He said signs would occur in Israel, society, nature, and the church. Jesus also cited rampant rebellion as an indication of the coming end.

> And because lawlessness will abound, the love of many will grow cold.
> —MATTHEW 24:12

Most read this and think, "Sure, rebellion abounds in our society." Yet in this passage Jesus was speaking to Christians. (See verses 10–11.) The Greek word for *love* in this verse is *agape*. This Greek New Testament word is used to describe the love of God, which is found in believers of Jesus Christ. It is the love only He can give. The world does not possess this kind of love. Jesus was saying, "Because disobedience will abound even among believers, the love of God in their hearts will grow cold!"

The mystery of lawlessness (rebellion) seduces society and believers alike. It gives Satan and his cohorts legal access to our homes, churches, institutions and governments.

THE GOOD NEWS

The good news is that many who are held captive will be set free as the tyranny and deception of lawlessness are exposed. They will not remain captives of the devil to do his will. God will reveal the schemes of the enemy to those who truly love Jesus, and they will be delivered from his control.

Those who love the truth will not be deceived by this mystery of lawlessness (2 Thess. 2:10). Overcomers will embrace obedience and shun a self-serving life, for their delight is seeing God's will and purpose accomplished.

5

No Witchcraft,
Except...

No curse can be released against the obedient.

WHEN I PASTORED a youth group, I received a very interesting testimony. It came from Brad,* an on-fire fifteen-year-old. He had come to our youth service for the first time when he was fourteen. He came to me and said, "I want God!" His hunger touched the heart of God, and that very evening God's power transformed his life.

He was the junior varsity quarterback and dated the most popular girl in his school. Immediately after he was saved he broke up with

---

* Not his real name

his girlfriend. When she asked him why, he explained, "I'm serving Jesus now, and I know you don't want to."

He became one of the most on-fire youth in our group. It was not unusual for Brad and another young man his age to meet at four o'clock in the morning and pray together until it was time to get ready for school.

It was a year later when he excitedly came to me, "Pastor John, you have to hear what happened to me in school today!"

As previously stated, the occult involvement was heavy in the local high schools. Several of our young people had experienced direct confrontations with classmates involved in it.

"OK, Brad," I said, "Tell me what happened."

He said, "This short kid came up to me in school today and said, 'I'm going to put a curse on you!' When he said that I just started laughing. I didn't plan it; I just laughed.

"Then this kid got frustrated with me and said, 'I'm going to put a curse on you, and you will die in two days!' I laughed harder.

"He got all upset and began to yell, 'I'll put a curse on you, and you'll die now if you don't stop!' but I laughed even harder.

"Then all of a sudden, we were joined by a much larger, older boy. He shoved the smaller one aside and said, 'Get going.' Then he turned and said to me, 'He's new at this. He doesn't know what he is doing.' I stopped laughing and started thinking, *What is going on?*

"Then this big guy said, 'He doesn't realize you're one of those marked ones we can't touch because the God you serve is bigger than the god we serve.'

"So I said to the big guy, 'Why don't you give your life to Jesus?'

"He shook his head, 'I can't. I'm in this too far,' and walked away."*

When a person walks in obedience to God, witchcraft has no power over him. Satan is confined to darkness (Jude 6), so he has no access to us when we are joined with God, in whom is no darkness at all (1 John 1:5).

---

* Of course he had been deceived; he could have escaped, for there is none too lost for the blood of Jesus!

The effects of witchcraft are obvious in our society. Though subtle, they are no less real in the church. This chapter will address when a believer is protected against witchcraft—and when he is not!

A BLESSING RATHER THAN A CURSE

During their wilderness journey the children of Israel camped on the plains of Moab. They had just attacked and defeated Bashan. Earlier they had destroyed the Amorites because they would not allow the Israelites to pass through their territory.

Now as they camped in the midst of Moab, Balak, the king of Moab and Midian, was worried. His kingdom quaked in fear at the multitude of Israelites. They knew Israel had destroyed every nation that opposed them.

So King Balak sent word to the prophet Balaam. Balaam was renowned for his spiritual accuracy and insight. The king knew whatever Balaam prophesied happened. If he blessed, they were blessed; if he cursed, they were cursed.

After receiving two sets of ambassadors, Balaam consented to accompany the king to see if he could curse the children of Israel. He had been won over by the king's offer of money and honor. But Balaam warned the king that he was restricted to speak only the words God placed in his mouth.

The next day they climbed the high places of Baal so Balaam could observe the nation of Israel. After Balaam had assessed them, he instructed the king to erect seven altars and prepare sacrifices for each of them. Then Balaam opened his mouth to curse Israel, but instead he pronounced a blessing over them.

Needless to say the king was very upset. "What have you done to me? I took you to curse my enemies, and look, you have blessed them bountifully!" (Num. 23:11).

So Balaam suggested they move to a higher level in the hope of giving Balak what he wanted. Again they erected seven altars and offered additional sacrifices. But when Balaam opened his mouth he again blessed Israel instead of cursing them.

This entire process was repeated two more times. Each time Balaam attempted to curse but was compelled by God to bless Israel. In Balaam's second oracle we find this profound statement:

> He has not observed iniquity in Jacob,
> Nor has He seen wickedness in Israel.
> The LORD his God is with him,
> And the shout of a King is among them.
> God brings them out of Egypt;
> He has strength like a wild ox.
> For there is no sorcery against Jacob,
> Nor any divination against Israel.
>
> —NUMBERS 23:21–23

Israel walked in covenant with God. His mighty arm had delivered them from Egyptian oppression, symbolizing freedom from this world system and power. They were a forgiven and cleansed nation, baptized as they passed through the Red Sea. Therefore God said He observed no iniquity in them.

Balaam declared that because of Israel's covenant with God there was no sorcery or divination that could prosper against them. You could also state the principle this way:

> There is no witchcraft that works against God's people, nor any divination against His church!

We should encourage ourselves with this promise. Let the witches and warlocks rant, rave, and burn their candles. Let them recite their hexes, spells, and curses—not one can harm a child of God! They will not prevail against the church of the living God. Proverbs 26:2 says, "Like a fluttering sparrow or a darting swallow, an undeserved curse does not come to rest" (NIV).

"HOW CAN I CURSE WHOM GOD HAS NOT CURSED?"

Balaam observed, "How shall I curse whom God has not cursed?" (Num. 23:8). When David was attacked, he wrote:

Hide me from the secret plots of the wicked,
From the rebellion of the workers of iniquity,
Who sharpen their tongue like a sword,
And bend their bows to shoot their arrows—bitter words,
That they may shoot in secret at the blameless.
—PSALM 64:2–4

Curses may be released against the righteous, but they will not rest upon him. Watch what happens to those who release curses:

But God shall shoot at them with an arrow;
Suddenly they shall be wounded.
So He will make them stumble over their own tongue.
—PSALM 64:7–8

Notice they stumble over their own tongue. The very words they release to hurt others will circle back upon them. In another metaphor David explained it this way. "They have dug a pit before me; into the midst of it they themselves have fallen" (Ps. 57:6).

Even if Balaam had pronounced curses over the children of Israel, it only would have returned upon his own head. Balaam knew it was impossible to bring a witchcraft curse on God's people, even though he wanted to. Moses later reminded Israel, "They hired against you Balaam the son of Beor from Pethor of Mesopotamia, to curse you. Nevertheless the LORD your God would not listen to Balaam, but the LORD your God turned the curse into a blessing for you, because the LORD your God loves you" (Deut. 23:4–5). Hallelujah!

BALAAM'S COUNSEL

Balaam's blessings made King Balak furious. He exclaimed, "I called you to curse my enemies, and look, you have bountifully blessed them these three times! Now therefore, flee to your place. I said I would greatly honor you, but in fact, the LORD has kept you back from honor" (Num. 24:10–11).

The king was planning to give Balaam a great monetary reward and honor for cursing his enemies. But in essence the king told Balaam, "You can forget the reward. Your God obviously doesn't want you to have it. So get out of my sight."

As soon as Numbers finishes the story of Balaam and Balak, we read an amazing thing.

> Now Israel remained in Acacia Grove, and the people began to commit harlotry with the women of Moab. They invited the people to the sacrifices of their gods, and the people ate and bowed down to their gods. So Israel was joined to Baal of Peor.
> —NUMBERS 25:1–3

What happened to this nation that had served the Lord? The Book of Revelation says that Balaam "taught Balak to put a stumbling block before the children of Israel, to eat things sacrificed to idols, and to commit sexual immorality" (Rev. 2:14; also see Num. 31:16).

I can just picture the scene. Balaam really wanted the king's money. So he said to the king, "I can't curse them with my mouth or any other form of divination, but I can tell you how to get them under a witchcraft curse!"

King Balak said, "How can it be done?"

Balaam said, "Send your women and have them infiltrate Israel's camp. Have them bring their idols with them as well. This rebellion will bring them under a witchcraft curse."

Israel's disobedience caused a nation that could not be cursed to come under a severe plague. "The anger of the LORD was aroused against Israel...And those who died in the plague were twenty-four thousand" (Num. 25:3, 9). This was the greatest single loss Israel experienced in the wilderness, and it was all a result of their rebellion.

Radical disobedience opened the door to a radical plague. Their rebellion was so blatant that one Israelite man openly flaunted his sin with a Midianite woman in the sight of Moses and the entire congregation of Israel.

So what stopped the plague? You may have guessed—radical obedience!

> Now when Phinehas the son of Eleazar, the son of Aaron the priest, saw it [the man flaunting the Midianite woman], he rose from among the congregation and took a javelin in his hand; and he went after the man of Israel into the tent and thrust both of them through, the man of Israel, and the woman through her body. So the plague was stopped among the children of Israel.
>
> —NUMBERS 25:7–8

Allow me to point out that God is not the author of plagues and diseases. The children of Israel had blatantly rebelled and breached His covering of protection. The door was opened, so the enemy came in with his curse.

Once again this affirms that rebellion is witchcraft. It gives legal entrance to Satan's control. Israel escaped the curse of a soothsayer only to be decimated by its own disobedience.

A NEW TESTAMENT EXAMPLE

We've seen rebellion bring the people of the Old Testament under a witchcraft curse; now let's examine this principle in the New Testament. The apostle Paul wrote a stern letter to the Galatians (Gal. 1:2). Notice this letter was addressed to the churches, not the general populace of Galatia. Paul chided:

> O foolish Galatians! Who has bewitched you that you should not obey the truth before whose eyes Jesus Christ was clearly portrayed among you as crucified?
>
> —GALATIANS 3:1

God had revealed His salvation by grace to these churches by Paul's preaching. But it was not long before they began to disobey what once was clear to them. They turned to follow another gospel…one of works (Gal. 3:1, 16). However, this specific act of disobedience is not what I want to focus on. What is important is the fact that God had clearly revealed His will to them, and they turned from it to follow the reasoning of another. This reasoning bewitched them to the point of confusion.

Paul warned this church that they were under the influence of witchcraft. Some may question, "I thought there was no divination or witchcraft against God's people?" That is correct; no curse can be released against the obedient. But remember, rebellion or disobedience places a person under witchcraft.

Now let me make this point clear. We come under bewitchment when we disobey what God has made clear to us—not when we disobey what has not been revealed to us. What they disobeyed had been clearly revealed to the Galatians.

LEARNING OBEDIENCE THE HARD WAY

When I first began in the ministry, God instructed me, "John, don't do things in your ministry just because other ministries do it." I realized other ministries could do something and it would be the right decision for them, but it would be wrong for me to pattern my ministry after theirs if God hadn't told me to do the same!

The next point He emphasized to me was, "If an opportunity arises for the ministry, don't accept it just because it looks good. Find out if it is My will." Though He made this point as clear as the first, I did not absorb this point as well. I learned this one the hard way.

We had been traveling for only a few years. The major thrust of the messages I preached was God's purpose for times of spiritual dryness. Many lives were strengthened by this message. I felt God telling me to write a book on not only what I had been preaching but also living. We self-published this message in the book, *Victory in the Wilderness.*

A publisher became aware of this message. One of their top acquisitions men called our office. He told me he believed it was an urgent message for the body of Christ. He said, "John, we believe in the message God has given you, and we want to help you get it to the people." He then expressed his company's interest in republishing the book.

We spoke for thirty minutes. He told me all the different ways they could get our message out. They worked with all the top distributors and could give our book a potential position in every Christian bookstore. He told me they would spend thousands of dollars on advertising. He cited examples of other unknown authors and how their messages had now exploded across America as a result of their publishing influence.

As I hung up, I felt uneasy because God was already showing me I was not to do it. I had come to know His voice, especially when He was saying no.

I spoke to my wife about it. We both agreed, even though the offer sounded so good, to follow the lead of our hearts, which was to say no. Later I prayed, but even then my outlook did not change. Deep inside I knew it was not God's will.

The next day their acquisitions man called me again. Though I knew it was not God's will, I wanted to hear what he had to say. Though I wouldn't admit it at the time, this was an initial indication of trouble. Why should I listen when God had already shown me it was not His will?

Looking back I know the reason. It all sounded so good that I was flattered. I knew God had called me to bring this message to America. He'd shown me what would be entrusted to me. It was not a local or regional call; I felt a national mandate. Yet we had labored in the ministry for years without an avenue to the nation. I thought, *This could promote the message to a national level, thus opening increasingly effective doors to reach out to the nation. Am I missing an opportunity I might never have again?*

My reasoning began to cloud and overshadow the clear direction from God I had received only the day before. I continued to reason, *Am I being about this? This is an open door of opportunity. Why say no to something that would get God's Word proclaimed?*

Because I did not discourage him, this man continued to call me every other day for the next two weeks. The longer I listened, the more sense it seemed to make to publish our book with them. I came to the point where there was no longer a hesitation in my spirit. I had allowed reasoning and flattery to silence God's still, small voice. That left me in a dangerous position—I had convinced myself what was once denied by God was now His will.

My wife is the treasurer of our ministry, so I made plans for her to fly to the publisher's office to sign the contract. I was excited about the opportunity. However, the night before she left, two of our children began to vomit violently. When the second child became ill about 3:30 a.m., my wife looked at me and said, "John, I don't think I should go tomorrow. I think we're making a mistake. God has allowed this in order to get our attention."

I responded, "No way. This is the devil trying to stop it. He doesn't want us to go through with the publishing agreement. You need to go. I'll take care of the children." Even though she disagreed, she boarded the plane the next morning and signed the contract.

I had disobeyed what God had originally shown me. From that day forward all hell broke out against me. The door was now open due to my disobedience. The enemy let me have it.

THE DOOR WAS NOW OPEN

Since I'd been saved I had been blessed to have virtually no sickness or health problems (to God be the glory). My wife used to make comments like, "You never get sick!" I rarely caught anything, and if I did, it was over in twenty-four hours. Jesus provided divine health as well as forgiveness of sins when He died on the cross (Isa. 53:4–5, AMP). But from the day we signed that contract I fought sickness and couldn't shake it.

It started out with throwing up along with my children the night the contract was signed. It was only the second time in my adult life I'd vomited. A week later I was over the flu only to catch a virus. My wife and I had gone out of town to celebrate an anniversary. For days my temperature hovered between 101 and 102 degrees. Later in the week I preached while still sick with a high fever and the chills.

The fever continued on into the next week as I conducted meetings in Canada. I would preach with a high fever and return to my room to shiver under the covers with a temperature. I spent my days in bed or resting in chairs or couches.

The fever progressed into the third week. My wife and I couldn't believe what was happening. I had never fought sickness like this. I finally went to the doctor. He prescribed an antibiotic, and within a few days I was back to normal again.

But a week after I finished the antibiotics I caught a severe cold. I was miserable with a sore throat, stuffed head, and all the other annoying conditions. It dragged on for a week.

Less than two weeks after recovering from my cold, I injured my knee climbing a wall. The injury was so severe it put me in a wheelchair, and then I limped with a brace for several weeks. Then it was another month before I could walk normally.

As if all this wasn't enough, a few weeks later I was hit with another bout of virus. It was as bad as the first one, and once again I had to get a prescription to get over it. It seemed I couldn't go more than a week without some kind of sickness. This cycle lasted three and a half months. Through all this my wife did not become ill.

During all of this I was having all kinds of problems with the publisher. It seemed we couldn't agree on anything. Everything in the relationship was stressed. There was no flow in the project.

All this was accompanied by problems in other areas of my life—all which seemed impossible to resolve.

Enemy Access Denied

Since I'd been saved and especially since I'd been in ministry I had faced several trials, afflictions, and hardships. But this was altogether different. I prayed, battled the enemy with the Word of God, and confessed God's Word frequently, yet to no avail. What had always produced breakthroughs and victory before now only left me in a state of frustration.

Thank God for Repentance

With the passage of time, I knew I had missed God. I repented of my disobedience but still felt trapped. My wife and I knew we needed a miracle to get out of the contract. We joined hands and asked God to forgive me. Then together we asked the Lord to get us out of the mess I had created by my disobedience.

Within a couple of weeks the publisher wrote me and requested we cancel the contract. They were frustrated, too, and felt the project had become too difficult to work through. I was relieved. God's will was restored. But it came with a price. The entire ordeal ended up costing us approximately four thousand dollars and three and a half months of frustration. We had incurred all the expense and were left with nothing to show for it. It was an exhausting and costly lesson.

A few months later my wife and I were discussing all that happened. We suddenly linked all the sickness I had battled to my disobedience. Looking back we realized as soon as I had repented I was restored to my previous health. All the other problems that had loomed over us without resolve cleared away as well. I know that God did not put the sickness and other turmoil on me. Rather, I had opened my life to oppression by my disobedience. I had known what was right and had chosen my own will over God's. When I submitted to God, I then could resist the devil and his door of torment was shut!

Tragic Consequences of Disobedience

I have met many in the church who live in disobedience. Their lives consist of one crisis after another. There is always some problem they just can't seem to get victory in. They escape one to find themselves in another. Each scenario seems to become progressively worse. These problems consume their time, energy, and livelihood.

I have watched while their marriages end in divorce. They are passed over for promotions or, worse, even lose their jobs. They fall victim to theft, financial crisis, and tragedy. Frustrated, they frantically look for someone to blame—it is the fault of their husband, wife, parent, pastor, boss, government, or any other. Yet the truth is this: somewhere a door stands open, making them vulnerable to an onslaught of demonic oppression and attack.

There are two culprits at work that actually feed off each other. The first is deception. This darkness is found in their hearts because they have not obeyed God's Word (James 1:22). The second culprit is the tangled snare of controlling spirits who are sanctioned to attack at will because of disobedience. The paradox: because the people are deceived, they blame everything except their own disobedience. This blinds them to exactly what is needed to secure their freedom.

Thank God for His Word. Its light exposes deception by discerning the thoughts and intentions of our hearts (Heb. 4:12). David said it this way, "Before I was afflicted I went astray, but now I keep Your word...It is good for me that I have been afflicted, that I may learn Your statutes" (Ps. 119:67, 71).

Unfortunately, when some are afflicted due to disobedience they refuse to learn. They continue wandering in the wilderness of disobedience. They blame everyone else instead of learning from their error.

I must stop here to clarify a point. Every time a person faces difficulty, problems, or hardships it is not necessarily the product of disobedience. It is a fact that many suffer while in obedience to God.

Joseph was just such a man. He was not disobedient. Yet he spent years in slavery even though he was born free. Then he spent over two years in Pharaoh's dungeon—not as a result of disobedience but as the result of obedience to God. He fled sexual immorality, shunning seduction. Obedience increased his hardship. But even as he suffered, men could still perceive God's favor on his life. It was evidenced by Joseph's godly fear and obedience (Gen. 39:2–3, 21–23).

Cain also suffered but for a totally different reason. Offended, he refused to repent of his disobedience. This resulted in a curse over his life. He lived his years on the earth as a fugitive and a vagabond. His aimless and hopeless wanderings were an example to the generations that followed him. It was a warning of the price of refusal to repent and obey God.

THE BLESSING COMES AFTER OBEDIENCE

There is great blessing when a person truly repents of disobedience. Joel cried, "Return to the Lord your God, for He is gracious and merciful, slow to anger, and of great kindness; and He relents from doing harm. Who knows if He will turn and relent, and leave a blessing behind Him" (Joel 2:13–14).

It was just a short while after I repented of my folly with the publishing company offer that God turned everything around. Charisma House publishers asked me to do a book with them. With this offer there was great joy and life in my spirit. This time I knew in my heart it was God. I still prayed to confirm what I witnessed in my heart. It was then God spoke to me, "The other publisher was your idea. Charisma House is Mine."

The book you hold is our fourth book with them. Our working relationship has been a blessing. Through it God did more in the first two years than I ever hoped for or expected with the first book. It has not only been good for us but also for the kingdom. It is the blessing of obedience.

6

THE STRENGTH
OF REBELLION

THE REBELLIOUS SEE GOD'S WORD AS A RESTRAINING LAW RATHER THAN AS PROTECTION AND LIFE.

WHY WOULD ANYONE disobey God when they know His will? This is an important question to answer, for it reveals the motivations of our hearts.

I HAVE NEVER BEEN UNDER THE LAW!

A few years ago as I read through my New Testament, the following scripture leapt out at me and riveted my spirit:

> The sting of death is sin, and the strength of sin is the law.
> —1 CORINTHIANS 15:56

Examine carefully the second section of this scripture: "the strength of sin is the law." Before this scripture came alive in my heart I had always assumed that the strength of sin, lawlessness, or rebellion was the devil or the carnal nature of the flesh. It never occurred to me that sin received its strength from the law.

Inspired, I searched another familiar scripture: "For when we were in the flesh, the sinful passions which were aroused by the law were at work in our members to bear fruit to death" (Rom. 7:5). In meditating on this, I quickly saw that it is the law that arouses the passion or desire to rebel because rebellion gets its strength from the law! Without law there could be no rebellion.

Now you may wonder, *How would this apply to a twentieth-century Gentile Christian. I live under grace. I've never been under the law.*

Or have you? Do any of these sound familiar: I can't sleep in because I have to attend church tomorrow...I haven't read my four chapters in the Bible today...I had better have my devotion time...I can't do this or watch that because I'm a Christian.

Or perhaps others: Do I have to pay tithes off the gross or the net?...Am I allowed to divorce my wife if we're not in love anymore?...Am I allowed to drink? Can I date? As a Christian can I do such and such?

Better yet, ask yourself: Do you feel pressured to fulfill religious requirements in order to remain under God's blessing? Do you obey due to the fear of the consequences you might face if you didn't? If you have, these are symptoms of a life under the law!

WHY DO YOU NEED TO PRAY ABOUT IT?

To illustrate let's look again at Balaam. The king of Moab sent ambassadors requesting Balaam to curse Israel. These elders promised Balaam honor and wealth. The prophet responded, "Lodge here tonight, and I will bring back word to you, as the LORD speaks to me" (Num. 22:8). Notice Balaam used the term Lord. He was not a prophet of Baal or another god. He was a prophet of Jehovah, and he called Him Lord.

God came to Balaam with a question, "Who are these men with you?" (v. 9). God was saying, "Balaam, you know who these people are. Why are you even entertaining them or their request? They want to curse My people. Is not My answer obvious? Why does their offer to 'bless you' blind your eyes?"

There are some things we don't need to pray about. When presented with an opportunity that benefits us while compromising God's will or the safety or benefit of others, we should not need to ask God, a counselor, our pastor, or another minister!

Nevertheless the Lord was gracious to Balaam, instructing him in clear and certain terms, "You shall not go with them; you shall not curse the people, for they are blessed" (v. 12). Now there could be no doubt as to what was God's will.

RELUCTANT OBEDIENCE

The next morning Balaam brought his report to the princes of Balak. "Go back to your land, for the LORD has refused to give me permission to go with you" (v. 13).

"The Lord refused," he said. Doesn't this sound like a child who longs to go out and play with his friends but Mother or Father has said no? Sullen, he goes to the door and in a forlorn tone mumbles, "My parents won't let me play." His parents' words are the law that restrains him, and he resents it. In the same way, Balaam saw the word of the Lord as a restriction or law to him.

When Balak heard Balaam's response, he refused to accept it as a final answer. He sent more prominent and influential elders and upped the ante. They brought this new report to Balaam: "Balak will do anything you want him to."

Now, if your next door neighbor offered you anything he possessed, it would most likely not compare to what the king of a prosperous nation could give. This was quite a handsome offer for Balaam.

But Balaam stayed strong and boldly responded, "Though Balak were to give me his house full of silver and gold, I could not go beyond the word of the LORD my God, to do less or more" (v. 18).

He sounded strong—but not for long. His motive is revealed in his next statement, "Now therefore, please, you also stay here tonight, that I may know what more the LORD will say to me" (v. 19).

Was something unclear the first time? What more would he need to hear? God had been very precise and certain the first time around: "You shall not go with them."

Was more money going to change God's mind? Can you imagine God telling him, "Oh, Balaam, I can see you are going to be blessed. I was only having you hold out for a better offer. Go ahead now and go with them!" How absurd!

GOD'S WORD IS RESTRAINING BALAAM

Review Balaam's response. "Though Balak were to give me his house full of silver and gold, I could not go beyond the word of the LORD my God, to do less or more." Notice the key phrase, "I could not," instead of, "I will not." By this he indicates again that God's word was a law, hindrance, or restraint to him. It certainly was not his delight.

Balaam had enough spiritual wisdom to know he could not go beyond what the Lord said and remain under the shelter of God's blessing. Today there are still those who attend church and obey the Word of the Lord but only for the same reason as Balaam. They serve the Lord in order to receive His benefits, such as heaven and blessing in their life on earth. They call Him Lord yet are only willingly obedient when it is to their advantage.

They have just enough spiritual sense to get them in trouble. Knowing they can't disobey God and remain blessed, they search for a loophole in order to do their own will with the permission of God. They seek the counsel of pastors, counselors, and other believers, any who are God's mouthpiece. They want to be told what they want to hear.

HAS GOD CHANGED HIS MIND?

When Balaam went to God a second time, the response was different. God told him, "If the men come to call you, rise and go with them; but only the word which I speak to you—that you shall do" (v. 20).

God changed His mind! Now Balaam could go! Perhaps Balaam's reasoning was sound after all. Maybe God was having him hold out for a better offer.

The next morning Balaam got up, armed with God's permission to go. He saddled his donkey and left with the princes of Moab.

"Then God's anger was aroused because he went, and the Angel of the LORD took His stand in the way as an adversary against him" (vv. 22). What is wrong here? First God said no, then He said yes, and then He became angry with Balaam when he went! Why did God keep changing His mind?

God did not change His mind! He knew Balaam's heart was set on going. So God granted him permission.

This is a principle that every believer should grasp and understand. When we pester the Lord after He has already clearly shown His will, He may step back and allow us to have our way even though it does not correspond with His original plan. When our hearts are set on a course of action, God will grant us permission, though He knows we will later answer for the course we choose.

YOU WILL GET WHAT YOU ARE DETERMINED TO HAVE

We find several examples of this in Scripture. Israel was supernaturally supplied manna in the desert. It was so potent and nutritious that after eating two cakes of it, Elijah could travel for forty days and nights (1 Kings 19:5–8)! However, the children of Israel became weary of manna as their daily diet.

> Now the mixed multitude who were among them yielded to intense craving; so the children of Israel also wept again and said:

73

> "Who will give us meat to eat? We remember the fish which we
> ate freely in Egypt, the cucumbers, the melons, the leeks, the
> onions, and the garlic; but now our whole being is dried up; there
> is nothing at all except this manna before our eyes!"
>
> —NUMBERS 11:4–6

They requested some meat and God granted their desire by sending them quail. "He gave them their own desire. They were not deprived of their craving" (Ps. 78:29–30). "But while the meat was still between their teeth, before it was chewed, the wrath of the LORD was aroused against the people, and the LORD struck the people with a very great plague" (Num. 11:33).

Who gave them the meat? It was God! Yet He became angry as they ate what He had provided, and they came under judgment (Ps. 78:31). The reason was much deeper than eating. God had looked beyond their request and into their hearts. What He found was rebellion, a people with their hearts set on what they craved. They despised God's supernatural provision and gave themselves over to their own desires.

There was another price paid for this request. It seems this new diet fed their flesh but depleted their souls.

> And He gave them their request, but sent leanness into their soul.
>
> —PSALM 106:15

A literal translation says: "He [God] . . . sent wasting into their souls."[1] It was this leanness or wasting of soul that left them too weak to possess the Promised Land. Yes, God will give you what you want, but at what cost to you? He is sovereign but does not force His will on you. He desires children who trust that His way is best for them. Then they willingly submit to His ways, obeying cheerfully, not grudgingly!

Another example of this was found when Israel wanted a king. Samuel brought this request before God who answered that it was not His will. God forewarned of all the hardship that a king would cause.

He will take a tenth of your sheep. And you will be his servants. And you will cry out in that day because of your king whom you have chosen for yourselves.

—1 Samuel 8:17–18

"Nevertheless the people refused to obey the voice of Samuel; and they said, 'No, but we will have a king over us, that we also may be like all the nations'" (1 Sam. 8:19–20). God did not want them to be like all the other nations; He wanted them as His own. They complained and murmured, and God gave them what they wanted, even though He knew they would suffer under the rule of many a wicked king. And indeed they did suffer.

Another example is the parable of the prodigal son. He requested his inheritance before the appointed time of his father. The father knew what would happen to the wealth he had built and safeguarded once it was placed in the hands of his immature son. Yet the father did not deny his son's request but gave him his inheritance. Soon penniless, this son ended up in a pig pen.

These are but a few examples that illustrate the actions and consequences of the folly you face when your heart is set contrary to God's will. Though He may grant your request, it is not without some loss.

"I HAVE SINNED!"

Let's pick up our story of Balaam again. Balaam was riding his donkey on his way to try to curse Israel when "the Angel of the Lord took His stand in the way as an adversary against him" (Num. 22:22).

After a few mishaps with his donkey the Lord opened Balaam's eyes, and he saw the angel with a drawn sword. The angel said to Balaam, "Behold, I have come out to stand against you, because your way is perverse before Me" (v. 32).

Balaam saw that he was about to be judged: "I have sinned, for I did not know You stood in the way against me" (v. 34). He was sorry—but not because he had broken faith with God's original instruction. No—he feared the consequence he faced. His sorrow

75

was not godly but self-serving and left him open to fall deeper into deception.

"For godly sorrow produces repentance leading to salvation, not to be regretted; but the sorrow of the world produces death" (2 Cor. 7:10). Both sorrows apologize; both say, "I have sinned"; both can shed tears. However, only one leads to life. What's the difference? The sorrow of the world focuses on the consequences of disobedience. Godly sorrow focuses on the fact it has grieved the heart of God, the very One who loves us.

The nature of King Saul's sorrow, for example, was obvious. It was not until there was no one left to blame that he responded: "I have sinned; yet honor me now, please, before the elders of my people and before Israel" (1 Sam. 15:30).

He acknowledged his sin, as often happens when one is caught with his back to the wall. However, it was a selfish or self-serving sorrow. He was concerned how this exposé would appear to his elders and the men of Israel. He was not concerned about how his actions disappointed God.

He had executed his own agenda. God's command restrained him from enjoying the results of his disobedience. God's word had become restrictive law, not a delight to Saul. This condition of his heart led him further into deception.

Baalam's attitude was similar. He too had an agenda contrary to God's will. When confronted, he also acknowledged his sin, but his sorrow focused on the fact he had been caught and was about to be judged.

> And Balaam said to the Angel of the LORD, "I have sinned, for I
> did not know You stood in the way against me. Now therefore,
> if it displeases You, I will turn back."
>
> —NUMBERS 22:34

"If it displeases You"! What's it going to take? An angel comes out to kill him for his perverted way, and he is still trying to figure out if he can carry out his own agenda and stay in the confines of God's word. He views God's word as restrictive; therefore, it strengthens the rebellion in his heart.

GOD'S WORD—LAW OR LIFE?

Rebellion is exposed by our reaction to God's word. Is it delight or restraint? When the serpent twisted God's word in Eve's mind, it became law instead of life, and she disobeyed. Rebellion was aroused, and she died spiritually.

Moses' attitude toward God set him apart from the children of Israel. Moses hungered for God. He delighted in His way and word. The first time God manifested Himself to Moses as the great fire in the bush, Moses responded, "I will now turn aside and see this great sight" (Exod. 3:3). From that time on God was his life, his constant pursuit. God was the focus of Moses' heart whether God met him on the mountain or in the tabernacle of meeting.

In contrast, the children of Israel were only interested in what God could do for them. They did not hunger to know or please Him. They wanted to know how God was going to please them. Therefore God's word was a law to them. This heart attitude made them unable to obey Him for generations.

This mind-set will strengthen the temptation toward disobedience. A good example is people's reaction to God's word regarding abstinence until marriage. I have often heard about couples who commit fornication before marriage. Because they see God's guidelines as a restriction, not as protective, perfect wisdom, the law ignites their sexual desire for each other.

Reasoning takes over. *It can't be wrong. We are in love; therefore, it is pure. We are already joined together spiritually, and we'll marry eventually. I'm sure this is the right one for me. Why deny ourselves and wait for conventional marriage? We can experience the beauty of being one now.*

Law leads to lust, lust leads to reasoning, and reasoning leads to rebellion. They fully believe their reasoning is acceptable to God because they are deceived and in rebellion. The door is open for Satan to steal from them.

They may eventually marry, but then they find their sexual desire for each other wanes. It is lawful now, and the lust that had fueled their passion is gone. Their marriage has lost the pure desire God intended for it.

Conduct your own study through the Scriptures about rebellion. In each place you find rebellion you will observe that the word of God was viewed as restrictive by the rebellious individual. This is true not only of Scriptures but in our world today as well.

This leads us to the next portion of our study. If viewing God's word as a restraining law strengthens rebellion, what strengthens obedience?

7

THE STRENGTH OF OBEDIENCE

Out of an intense love for God, we take delight in fulfilling His will.

Two mighty forces strengthen us to obey God—love for God and fear of the Lord. Our life must exhibit both if we are to finish our race of obedience.

"If You Love Me..."

I was preparing to minister one evening and was in prayer. I was aware God desired to speak something to my spirit. I quieted myself before Him, and He spoke, "Read John 14:15."

By the reference alone I had no idea what John 14:15 said. So

Enemy Access Denied

I turned to it and noticed in my Bible it began a new paragraph. I read these words of Jesus: "If you love Me, keep My commandments."

I read from verse 15 down to verse 24. All ten of these verses related back to verse 15. After reading the last verse the Lord spoke to my heart, "You didn't get it. Read it again."

I read all ten verses again. What I heard through these scriptures was: "By keeping My commandments, you prove you love Me."

Again I heard His voice speak, "You didn't get it. Read it again." Now my curiosity was aroused. I read the ten verses again only to hear the Lord say, "You didn't get it. Read it again." This transpired a number of times until my frustration began to mount.

Exasperated, about the eighth time I cried, "Lord, please forgive my ignorance! Open my eyes to see what You're saying!"

Then I read verse 15 again: "If you love Me, †keep My commandments." I noticed a reference marker (†) by the word *keep*. I went to the reference notes in the margin and noted the more accurate translation was "you will keep." By substituting this phrase in the place of the single word keep the verse read, "If you love Me, you will keep My commandments."*

When I read it this way, skyrockets went off inside me. I saw what He was saying. "John, I wasn't saying if you keep My commandments, you will prove that you love Me. I already know whether you love Me or not! I was saying, if you fall head over heels in love with Me, you will be able to keep My commandments!" My original vantage point was the law; the new view is relationship.

If You Love Someone, You Show It

Have you ever fallen in love? When I was engaged to my wife, Lisa, I was head over heels in love with her. She was my constant thought. I'd do whatever I could just to spend time with her. If she needed something, no matter what the inconvenience, if at all possible, I

---

* I was reading from the New King James Version. Most other modern translations use the word *will* in the main text (see NIV, NAS).

would get it for her. If she had called me in the middle of the night and said, "Honey, I want ice cream," I would have said, "Do you want chocolate or vanilla? I'll be there in five minutes!" I would have done anything to fulfill any desire or request she made of me.

Because of my intense love for her, it was a joy to do whatever she wished. I didn't do this to prove I loved her; I did it because I loved her!

This exemplifies what Jesus was saying. Out of an intense love for Him, we take delight in fulfilling His desire. His word is not a restrictive law but our consuming passion!

"I Delight to Do Your Will"

In this light let's look at King David. David was a man who loved God with a passion. God said, "I have found David the son of Jesse, a man after My own heart, who will do all My will" (Acts 13:22). There was no willful rebellion in his life. What gave him the ability to do all of God's will? He delighted in God's commands. He did not see them as restraints but as bonds of his relationship with God.

David wrote often of the law!

> I will delight myself in Your commandments, which I love...Your testimonies also are my delight and my counselors.
> —Psalm 119:47, 24

> I will delight myself in Your statutes; I will not forget Your word.
> —Psalm 119:16

> Make me walk in the path of Your commandments, for I delight in it.
> —Psalm 119:35

> I delight to do Your will, O my God.
> —Psalm 40:8

Love Produces Genuine Repentance

David loved God; therefore, it was his delight to obey Him. However, there was a dark time period in his life, a season when he departed from this obedience. He took Bathsheba, wife of Uriah the Hittite, one of David's faithful soldiers. When David found out she was pregnant he tried to conceal it from her husband by bringing him home to sleep with her. When Uriah would not go to his wife because the other soldiers were still at the front lines, David had him murdered.

Once again a prophet was sent to confront a king. This time King David was confronted by the prophet Nathan. Nathan exposed David's treachery. He pronounced a judgment over David, "Now therefore, the sword shall never depart from your house...because by this deed you have given great occasion to the enemies of the LORD" (2 Sam. 12:10, 14). David's disobedience had opened the devil's door. It left his life and family vulnerable to the enemies of God—not only the natural ones but also the spiritual ones. A family and a nation would suffer by way of his disobedience.

In the midst of this intense confrontation David's love for God caused him to repent quickly and return to a life of obedience. He cried out before the prophet, "I have sinned against the LORD" (2 Sam. 12:13).

Both Saul and David confessed they sinned. Yet Saul was concerned for himself while David understood whose heart he had disappointed. Unlike Saul, David was not concerned with what his elders or men of Israel thought. He was alone before his God and only cared what God thought. He loved God more than anyone or anything. Knowing he'd hurt the heart of God, he would not allow himself to be comforted by man. He wanted to be reconciled to his Master.

And he cried out: "Against You, You only, have I sinned, and done this evil in Your sight" (Ps. 51:4). His heart was broken from the weight of disappointing the One he loved. It was the most painful consequence of his disobedience. Unlike Balaam, it was not the sword David feared; he could not stand the breach between his Lord and him.

David's son with Bathsheba died. His daughter was raped and defiled by her own brother. One son murdered another, then his favorite son rose up against him in rebellion, took the throne, and attempted to murder David. Then that son was killed. The price of David's disobedience was great, but God retained him as king.

David was after God's heart, while Saul was after a kingdom! David was sustained by his love for God; Saul was destroyed by his love for self. God's judgment of David's failure to keep His law did not cause David to rebel and view the law as impossible. Rather it caused him to love God even more passionately so that he would never fail Him again.

These two lives illustrate what the Lord revealed to me through John 14:15. When we love Jesus with all our hearts, we can obey Him. All else pales in comparison because nothing is more important. He becomes our life.

THE FEAR OF THE LORD

The second force that strengthens obedience is the fear of the Lord. Proverbs 16:6 says, "By the fear of the LORD one departs from evil." By the fear of the Lord men depart from disobedience.

Much can be learned by examining the children of Israel. Paul explained their experiences in the wilderness, "Now all these things happened to them as examples, and they were written for our admonition [instruction], upon whom the ends of the ages have come" (1 Cor. 10:11). We are to learn from their example.

They lost the promise of God due to their disobedience. Paul explained: "And to whom did He swear that they would not enter His rest, but to those who did not obey?" (Heb. 3:18).

Their disobedience was not due to a lack of knowledge. The word of God had been proclaimed to them. "For who, having heard, rebelled" (Heb. 3:16).

Why then did they disobey the God who had done so many mighty miracles and lived in their midst? God summed it up this way:

> Oh, that they had such a heart in them that they would fear Me and always keep all My commandments, that it might be well with them and with their children forever!
>
> —Deuteronomy 5:29

They did not fear God; therefore, they could not keep His commandments. The one who fears God will set his heart toward keeping all His commandments, not just the ones he selects or the convenient ones. To fear God is to tremble at His word. You will not take lightly anything God has said. Each command is honored as important.

Read carefully the following exhortation given to New Testament believers:

> Therefore, since a promise remains of entering His rest, let us fear lest any of you seem to have come short of it.
>
> —Hebrews 4:1

This verse admonishes us to fear lest we fall short of entering God's promise as the children of Israel did. How could a New Testament believer lose the promises of God? Paul says, "Let us therefore be diligent to enter that rest, lest anyone fall according to the same example of disobedience" (Heb. 4:11).

There is a link between disobedience and a lack of the fear of the Lord, just as obedience is paired with the fear of the Lord. We find the strength to obey hidden in the fear of the Lord.

> Therefore, having these promises, beloved, let us cleanse ourselves from all filthiness of the flesh and spirit, perfecting holiness in the *fear of God.*
>
> —2 Corinthians 7:1, emphasis added

He Tests Us by the Absence of His Presence

The fear of the Lord includes, but is not limited to, reverence and respect. It is to acknowledge Him with the glory, honor, and preeminence He alone possesses. When we hold this position in our hearts, we will esteem Him and His desire over and above our own desires. We will hate what He hates and love what He loves, trembling at His word and in His presence.

I believe God will withhold His glory to test and prepare us. Will we fear and obey Him even when His tangible presence is not manifest? So often the modern church behaves as foolishly as the children of Israel—rejoicing in His presence and miracles yet sinning when these things are absent.

The Israelites were excited when God blessed them and performed mighty miracles for them. When God parted the Red Sea and brought them across on dry ground, burying their enemies behind them, they sang, danced, and shouted the victory (Exod. 15:1–21). Sounds like a modern-day charismatic service!

But only a few days later when His power was not so apparent and food and drink were scarce, they complained against God and wanted to return to Egypt. They had quickly forgotten their captivity and decided slavery had been better for them (Exod. 16:3).

Later God came down in His awesome splendor on Mount Sinai, wrapped in a dark cloud to shield His brilliant glory. There was thundering, lightning, and earthquakes. We've yet to see this magnitude of glory!

God had come to speak to the children of Israel and Moses. Now they did not complain or disobey in His fearful presence—they were frightened and drew back from His awesome presence. Moses pleaded with them, "Do not fear; for God has come to test you, and that His fear may be before you, so that you may not sin" (Exod. 20:20). Notice Moses' words, "that you may not sin."

It is very important to note the difference between being afraid of God and fearing God. If people are afraid of God they run and hide from Him. They will not keep His word because they will not know His heart. The children of Israel retreated from God's glorious presence. Although they promised to keep His word (Exod. 24:13), for two thousand years they could not.

On the other hand, the one who fears God (but is not afraid of Him) will draw closer to Him: "So the people stood afar off, but Moses drew near the thick darkness where God was" (Exod. 20:21). Only as we draw near do we find the strength to obey. Many parents discover that the children who are closest to them are the most obedient.

You would think after experiencing all this glory, the children of Israel would obey, right? Wrong! While they drew away Moses went to the top of the mountain. With Moses gone, God's presence was not tangible. What did these people do? They took the gold God gave them from the Egyptian women and built a golden calf with it! Interesting isn't it? They took the blessing of God and made it an idol! (Have we in the church sometimes turned God's blessings into idols?) Again, it was a lack of the fear of God that produced their disobedience in God's absence.

A Totally Different Response

Joseph was quite a different story. God gave him a dream that showed him he would be a great leader. He would lead his brothers and even his mother and father. The children of Israel had a promise of a new land and Joseph had a promise of leadership. But what happened after he received this promise? The brothers over whom he ruled in his dream ended up throwing him into a pit. However, we find no evidence that Joseph complained against God.

Then he was sold as a slave into a foreign nation by these same brothers. He served as a slave in another man's house for over ten years. Though he was given a dream by God, each day, each year, he appeared to head in the opposite direction. Imagine his thoughts, *Where is God? Where is His promise?* Yet he fought these doubts and did not yield to them!

The children of Israel did not battle against these thoughts: They indulged in them. Though Joseph was patient for ten years, they were ready to quit in less than forty days! Many people have bitter thoughts toward God if their prayers aren't answered in two weeks. Quite different from Joseph, wouldn't you agree?

Joseph endured for more than ten years without even a hint of possible fulfillment of God's promise. He was isolated in a pagan land from all that he had known or loved. The wife of the man whom he had served faithfully cast longing eyes toward Joseph. She had a strong, seducing spirit and wanted him. Dressed in the finest of Egypt and wearing the best perfume, she knew how to seduce a man. She did not solicit him once but daily.

I love the way Joseph feared God. He did not disobey, though he had experienced hardship and disappointment. Joseph denied this attractive woman. "How then can I do this great wickedness, and sin against God?" (Gen. 39:9). Consistently he said no. This obedience to God eventually resulted in imprisonment in Pharaoh's dungeon. Even there he continued to fear God! No disappointment could draw this man's heart away from obedience to God.

We have preached messages in the church that would lead you to believe that if you're in hardship you are out of the will of God. Yet in obedience to God, Joseph suffered!

FEAR AND TREMBLING

It is clear that the fear of God yields the strength to obey while the lack of it leads to disobedience.

> Therefore, my beloved, as you have always obeyed, not as in my presence only, but now much more in my absence, work out your own salvation with fear and trembling; for it is God who works in you both to will and to do for His good pleasure.
> —PHILIPPIANS 2:12–13

I know this is a letter from Paul to the Philippians, but it is also a letter from the Lord to us. I like to read this verse as though God were speaking to me personally. It shows how the fear of God will strengthen me to obey Him not only in His presence but also in His absence. (I'm not writing of His departing from us, for He has said that He will not forsake us, but I am writing of the times when we don't feel Him or when His promises are yet to be fulfilled.)

89

God will work in those who fear Him so that they will both want to do His will and then actually do it. I hear many claim this promise, yet its benefits are limited to those who fear and tremble before the Lord Almighty.

There is such a weak understanding of the fear of the Lord. Many view it as an optional virtue in the New Testament or limit it to a reverence or respect for God. However, if all we need is respect, why does Paul describe "fear and trembling"? Trembling does not sound like mere respect.

If it meant only reverence, why did the writer of Hebrews admonish us, "Let us have grace, by which we may serve God acceptably with reverence and godly fear. For our God is a consuming fire" (Heb. 2:28–29). Believe me, the all-consuming fire inspires more than just reverence!

Heavenly Father—Consuming Fire

Our Father God, the great consuming fire, the One who placed the stars in the heavens with His fingers, merits much more awe than what we have given Him. How can we claim to know Him if we do not fear Him? The fear of the Lord is the beginning, the very onset, of knowing Him (Prov. 1:7; 2:5). You haven't truly begun to know Him until you acquire the fear of Him.

Yes, He loves us. He is love (1 John 4:8). But He is also a consuming fire (Heb. 12:29)! He is our Father (Rom. 8:15), but He is also the Judge of all (Heb. 12:23). Yes, we are to love Him, but we are to fear Him as well. We are admonished to "consider the goodness and severity of God" (Rom. 11:22).

Our ministry and obedience to Him is incomplete without both love and fear. "On some have compassion, making a distinction; but others save with fear, pulling them out of the fire, hating even the garment defiled by the flesh" (Jude 22–23).

Let us ask God to fill us with His love (Rom. 5:5) but not to the neglect of the Spirit of His holy fear (Isa. 11:2–3). These two forces will enable us to walk in obedience before Him.

8

GRACE THAT MISLEADS

GRACE IS NOT MERELY A COVER-UP.

OUR MODERN CHURCH has developed a deceptive thought process, one that has been conceived and brought forth by an unbalanced teaching of grace. Most often I hear grace referred to as an excuse or cover-up for a life of disobedience. To put it quite bluntly, it is used as a justification for self-seeking, fleshly lifestyles.

Many Christian circles have overemphasized the goodness of God to the neglect of His holiness and justice. This swing to the extreme left has caused many to lose their taste for the whole counsel of God. It is not unlike a child who is unaccustomed to a balanced diet because he only eats what he likes. The child is robbed not only of the taste of some foods but also the nutrition his body needs from them.

We will never develop an appetite for what we have not tasted. To remain balanced we are to "consider the goodness *and* severity of God" (Rom. 11:22, emphasis added). If our counsel is not balanced we have a tendency to develop a warped or bent understanding of God.

In conversation and from pulpits I have heard believers and leaders use grace and God's love as an excuse for disobedience. Grace is unmerited, and it does cover but not in the manner we've taught.

This lack of balance has infiltrated our thinking so completely we feel the liberty to disobey God whenever it is inconvenient for us. We assure ourselves that grace covers our disobedience. After all, God loves us and understands how busy we are, and He wants us happy at all costs! Right? Granted, we do not usually verbalize this thought process, yet it exists just the same.

Such thinking is validated by the fruit we see in the church. Unfortunately, it is not uncommon to find church members who are irreverent toward all forms of authority. They are self-willed, stubborn, insubordinate, and driven and controlled by their various lusts. They pursue the lifestyle and possessions of the world while calling them the blessings of the Lord. Unaware of their deception, they rest secure, lulled by a false sense of security based on the grace of God.

The grace of God is not merely a cover-up. Yes, it covers, but it goes beyond that—it enables and empowers us to live a life of obedience.

NOT MERELY A COVER-UP

Observe the standard God looks for in a believer's life. Jesus said:

> You have heard that it was said to those of old…But I say to you.
>
> —MATTHEW 5:21–22

Jesus used this pattern five more times in the rest of the chapter. First He quoted the requirement of the law of Moses with, "You have heard it said." Then He introduced what God seeks from a believer under the new covenant with, "But I say to you." In doing this He contrasted the Mosaic law with grace and truth.

> The law was given through Moses, but grace and truth came through Jesus Christ.
>
> —JOHN 1:17

This is why He said, "But I say to you." He introduced the dimension grace would impart to the law. One was an outside restraint while the other was an inward transformation.

Often I hear believers and ministers bemoan the harsh requirements of the law, then express their relief that they are under grace and not required to follow such a rigid lifestyle. Well, I also rejoice exceedingly that I am no longer under the law. But it is not because God's standard of obedience is so much more lenient now. His standard is higher under grace! Let's see what Jesus said about specific issues.

> You have heard that it was said to those of old, "You shall not commit adultery." But I say to you that whoever looks at a woman to lust [desire] for her has already committed adultery with her in his heart.
>
> —MATTHEW 5:27–28

A judgment of guilt was passed under the old covenant if an act of adultery was physically committed. In contrast, under the new covenant a guilty verdict is awarded if a man merely looks at a woman with desire in his heart. In plain language, under the law you had to do it—under the new covenant of grace, all you have to do is entertain the tempting thought!

Let's examine another comparison:

> You have heard that it was said to those of old, "You shall not murder, and whoever murders will be in danger of the judgment." But I say to you that whoever is angry with his brother

without a cause shall be in danger of the judgment. And whoever
says to his brother, "Raca!" . . . shall be in danger of hell fire.

—MATTHEW 5:21–22

The word *raca* can be roughly translated as "fool," but the actual
idea is really "you good-for-nothing moron!"[1] It was a term of
reproach commonly used among Jews at the time of Christ. If anger
reached the point where one called a brother a moron, Jesus said he
was in danger of hell.

In the Old Testament you were guilty of murder if you took a
physical life. Under the grace of the New Testament, God equates
anger against your brother with the severity of murder! First John
3:15 says, "Whoever hates his brother is a murderer, and you know
that no murderer has eternal life abiding in him."

Under the law you had to run a knife through someone. Under
grace if you refuse to forgive or if you allow prejudice or another
form of hatred to rule your heart, it is evidence that God's eternal
life or grace does not abide in you.

We have been deceived into believing that entrance to God's
kingdom is granted to the lawless of heart. Again, does this sound
like the grace we've lived and taught? We are tempted to view grace
as a big cover-up.

If grace is merely a cover-up, then Jesus contradicted the very grace
He came to impart.

But this is not true, for in Titus 2:11–12 we find, "For the grace of
God that brings salvation has appeared to all men, teaching us that,
denying ungodliness and worldly lusts, we should live soberly, righteously, and godly in the present age." Grace is the ability to live free
of ungodliness and worldly desire. In actuality it is the capability to
live a lifestyle of obedience.

The presence of outward, fleshly lusts is a manifestation of a
disobedient heart.

For this you know, that no fornicator, unclean person, nor
covetous man, who is an idolater, has any inheritance in the

kingdom of Christ and God. Let no one deceive you with empty words, for because of these things the wrath of God comes upon the sons of disobedience.

—Ephesians 5:5–6

Notice Paul referred to those who would not enter God's kingdom as "sons of disobedience." Their outward sin was rooted in a disobedient heart.

Cain's outward manifestations were anger, jealousy, and murder. But the root of these was his disobedience to God's authority.

SAVED BY GRACE

The writer of Hebrews exhorts, "Let us have grace, by which we may serve God acceptably with reverence and godly fear" (Heb. 12:28). Grace is a force that enables us to serve God acceptably. It is the essence of the power to live a life of obedience to God. This is the proof of our salvation. For we are told that Jesus "gave Himself for us, that He might redeem us from every lawless deed and purify for Himself His own special people, zealous for good works" (Titus 2:14).

In rebuttal, some may argue, "But the Bible says, 'By grace we have been saved through faith not of our own works. It is the gift of God.'" (See Ephesians 2:8–9.)

Yes, that is true. It is impossible to live a life worthy of our inheritance in the kingdom of God by our own strength, for all have sinned and fallen short of God's righteous standard (Rom. 3:23). None will ever be able to stand before God and claim that their works, charitable deeds, or good life has earned them the right to inhabit His kingdom. Every one of us has transgressed and deserves to burn in the lake of fire eternally.

God's answer for our shortcomings is salvation through His gift of grace! A gift cannot be earned! Romans 4:4 says, "Now to him who works, the wages are not counted as grace but as debt." If you work for it, it's not grace. Even if you did try to earn grace, you could never live well enough to get it. You could pour out your life in sacrifice and charitable works yet never earn this grace. It is a gift, and it is received through faith in Jesus.

Many in the church understand this. When Martin Luther received this revelation in the 1500s, it was so revolutionary that it brought forth the Reformation. The realization of the gift of grace brought many out of gross spiritual darkness. It is right to preach the strength of this truth as we have in both evangelical and Spirit-filled churches.

But we have failed to emphasize the power of grace not only to redeem us but also to grant us the ability to live in a new way. For the Word of God declares:

> Faith by itself, if it does not have works, is dead. But someone will say, "You have faith, and I have works." Show me your faith without your works, and I will show you my faith by my works.
> —James 2:17–18

Faith That Works

James was not contradicting Paul. He was rounding out or clarifying Paul's message. The evidence that a person has received God's gift of grace is a life of obedience to the Lord. A person who consistently disobeys God's Word is one in whom faith has never truly existed or it has failed. What? A person's faith can die? Absolutely! Jesus said to Peter, "But I have prayed for you, that your faith should not fail; and when you have returned to Me, strengthen your brethren" (Luke 22:32). If faith was unable to fail, why would Jesus have prayed in this manner?

Jesus warned His church, "Remember therefore from where you have fallen; repent and do the first works, or else I will come to you quickly and remove your lampstand from its place—unless you repent" (Rev. 2:5). He dealt with the fact their works had failed. He did not mention their intentions! O beloved, hear His Word and quit listening to the incomplete doctrines of mere men!

> You see then that a man is justified by works, and not by faith only.
>
> —JAMES 2:24

James prefaced this statement by using Abraham, the father of faith, as the example: "Was not Abraham our father justified by works [notice: justified by works] when he offered Isaac his son on the altar? Do you see that faith was working together with his works, and by works faith was made perfect? And the Scripture was fulfilled which says, 'Abraham believed God, and it was accounted to him for righteousness'" (James 2:21–23).

What happened here? Abraham *believed* God and therefore did the works that resulted in justification. In our day *belief* has been reduced to mental assent. Multitudes have prayed the sinner's prayer because they were moved emotionally, yet they returned to the path of disobedience. They continue to live for themselves, trusting in an intellectual salvation that never changed their hearts. Yes, they believe in God, but James said, "You believe that there is one God. You do well. Even the demons believe—and tremble!" (James 2:19). What good is it to acknowledge Jesus Christ without a change of heart and thus a change in actions?

In the Scriptures we find *believe* means not only to acknowledge the existence of Jesus but also to obey His will and His Word. Hebrews 5:9 says Jesus became "the author of eternal salvation to all who obey Him." To believe is to obey. The proof of Abraham's belief was in his corresponding works of obedience. He offered what was most precious to him. Nothing, not even his son, meant more to him than obeying God. This is true faith. It is why he is honored as the father of faith (Rom. 4:16). Do we see this faith evident in the church today? How have we been so deceived?

Just *saying* you have faith does not prove you actually do. How can faith be real without corresponding actions of obedience? Hear the words again: "You see then that a man is justified by works, and not by faith only" (James 2:24). Perhaps the day will come when the church will proclaim this scripture as loudly as it has Ephesians 2:8–9. Then it will be zealous, not floundering in a dangerous, lukewarm condition.

JESUS' MESSAGE TO HIS CHURCH IN THE LAST DAYS

The Book of Revelation holds messages to seven historical churches. But the application of these messages is not limited to these churches or they would not be included as Scripture. Each message holds a historic and prophetic application. Most theologians agree the seven churches represent a chronological pattern progressing from the early church unto the present and soon to be.

Though we do not know the day or the hour of His return, Jesus said we would know the season. Many agree we are living in the season of His return. Therefore the last word, Laodicea, would apply prophetically to us. First note, this letter was not written to the city of Laodicea, but to its church! Keep these things in mind as you read.

> And to the angel of the church of the Laodiceans write, "These things says the Amen, the Faithful and True Witness, the Beginning of the creation of God."
>
> —REVELATION 3:14

Jesus called Himself the Faithful and True Witness. Faithful means He is consistent and constant. True means He will only speak the truth, even if it is not delightful. Faithful and true means He will be consistently true, no matter what the reaction or pressure.

A false witness will lie and flatter. He tells only what you want to hear at the expense of what you need to hear. A dishonest salesman wants your money and will treat you very nicely and tell you just what you want to hear. But his motive is to take from you. As a church we have embraced ministries who have told us what we wanted to hear. We only wanted to hear nice and wonderful things to the neglect of the truth we needed.

Jesus comforts and builds but not at the terrible expense of neglecting to tell you the truth. He loves and forgives but also chastens and corrects! Hear His words:

> I know your works, that you are neither cold nor hot.
>
> —REVELATION 3:15

Notice He said works, not intentions. The road to hell is paved with good intentions. How did He know their condition? By their works or their actions.

The actions of those who are cold would be blatant disobedience to God. They do not pretend to be something they are not. They are lost and know it. They know they are not serving God. They serve other gods—their money, their business, themselves. They live for the pleasure of the moment in revelry and riot. Such is the life of a sinner or admitted backslider.

On the other hand, those who are hot are consumed with God. God encompasses their hearts and beings. It is their joy and delight to obey Him. They also know their true condition.

Jesus warned the last church their condition was neither cold nor hot. Now look at this next statement:

> I could wish you were cold or hot.
>
> —REVELATION 3:15

This statement bothered me. Why would Jesus say to a church, "I would rather you be cold or hot"? Why wouldn't He say, "I wish you were hot"? It is obvious that their present condition (somewhere between cold and hot) was more objectionable to God than being cold. How could an all-out sinner or acknowledged backslider be in a better position than these so-called church believers? He answers this with His next statement.

> So then, because you are lukewarm, and neither cold nor hot, I will vomit you out of My mouth.
>
> —REVELATION 3:16

What is lukewarm? It has too much hot to be cold and too much cold to be hot. Lukewarm is a blend. It has enough heat to blend in undetected with the hot and enough cool to slip in unnoticed with the cold. Lukewarm people become like whoever they are around. If around those obedient to the Lord they can blend in. They know the scriptures, sing the songs, and say the right statements and clichés.

When around the world they blend again. They might not drink or smoke, but they think and conduct their lives in a worldly manner: selfishly. They obey God when it is pleasant to or when it is in their best interests. But they are really motivated by their own desires.

Jesus said, "I will vomit you out of My mouth." Why did He choose this graphic analogy? To answer, we must know why a person vomits. We vomit what our body cannot assimilate. Recently, I took two of my sons to lunch. They both ordered hamburgers. Within the hour both of them had vomited their lunch. They had eaten bad meat and their bodies rejected it because it was not good for them. These bad hamburgers looked just like the good ones they had eaten before.

Jesus is saying, "I am going to vomit out of My body those who say they belong to Me but really don't."

The cold are not deceived, the hot are not deceived, but lukewarm people are deceived. They think their condition is something other than what it is. This is why God's judgment could be worse for them than for an all-out sinner. The sinner knows he is not serving God. Lukewarm people think they are. They confess salvation by grace but in actuality have fallen short of the very grace of God they confess (Heb. 12:15).

This makes them much more difficult to reach. Persons who think they are saved see no need for salvation. This is why Jesus goes into detail about their true condition.

> Because you say, "I am rich, have become wealthy, and have need of nothing"—and do not know that you are wretched, miserable, poor, blind, and naked.
>
> —Revelation 3:17

Without a doubt, they believed they were saved, secure, and on their way to heaven. Why should they repent? They confessed a born-again faith, but their lives confessed differently. Therefore, Jesus loved them enough to point out their deception.

NOT EVERYONE WHO SAYS, "LORD, LORD"

Not everyone who says they are saved by grace is. A true believer is not known by what he confesses but is known by his fruit of obedience.

> Therefore by their fruits you will know them. Not everyone who says to Me, "Lord, Lord," shall enter the kingdom of heaven, but he who does the will of My Father in heaven.
> —MATTHEW 7:20–21

Allow me to put these words into modern vernacular: "You will not know who is or who isn't a believer by what they profess but by their submission to My Father's will. Not everyone who says, 'I am a Christian; Jesus is my Lord,' will be granted entrance into heaven but only those who obey the will of the Father."

And again Jesus said:

> Many will say to Me in that day, "Lord, Lord, have we not prophesied in Your name, cast out demons in Your name, and done many wonders in Your name?" And then I will declare to them, "I never knew you; depart from Me, you who practice lawlessness!"
> —MATTHEW 7:22–23

In our modern vernacular: "A great number of people will confess Me as Lord and pray a sinner's prayer. Many of them consider themselves charismatic or Pentecostal. Yes, even those who did miracles and cast out demons in My name will be shocked at the realization of their true condition on that day. They expect an entrance to the kingdom of heaven only to hear Me say, 'Depart from Me, you who lived a life of lawlessness (disobedience to the will of God My Father).'"

This is not my account or my words. It is not pleasant to think there will be many who are denied admittance to the kingdom of heaven—even some who cast out demons and did miracles in His name.

The people who did wonders in Jesus' name had to have been saved at one time. Those who have never professed salvation in His name cannot do supernatural works in His name. There is an account of those who tried in the Book of Acts. The seven sons of Sceva took it upon themselves to call upon the name of the Lord Jesus to cast out an evil spirit in a man, saying, "We exorcise you by the Jesus whom Paul preaches." The evil spirit answered, "Jesus I know, and Paul I know; but who are you?" Then the demonized man leaped on the seven brothers, overpowered them, and drove them out of the house naked and wounded (Acts 19:13–16).

So we can see that nonbelievers are unable to cast out demons in Jesus' name, though they may attempt to do so by copying what true believers do. This reinforces the fact that in Matthew 7:22–23 Jesus was speaking of people who were denied entrance to heaven though they had followed Him at some point in their lives.

I received a sobering vision in the late 1980s that changed the course of my life and ministry. I saw a multitude of people, too great to number, the magnitude of which I had never seen before. They were amassed before the gates of heaven, awaiting an entrance. They expected to hear the Master say, "Come, you blessed of My Father, inherit the kingdom prepared for you from the foundation of the world" (Matt. 25:34). But instead the Master said, "I never knew you; depart from Me." God showed me the agony and terror on their faces. It had a riveting effect on my soul that has grown stronger over time.

Scriptures speak of two groups of people who expect entrance into the kingdom of heaven but will be denied:

1. Those who give their lives to Jesus for selfish purposes. They are more interested in the blessings than the

Blesser. From the start they are deceived because the cares, riches, and pleasures of this life choke out the Word they hear and confess. (See Luke 8:15.)

2. Those who convert with sincere motives but later lose their salvation. This group (which I believe is smaller than the first group) walks away from obedience to His lordship.

We'll look at the second group in the next chapter, and we'll turn to the first group now.

JOINED WITH JESUS

Again, those in the first group join themselves with Jesus solely for the benefits of salvation. Though they accept His salvation, they never come to know the heart of God. They only go as far as His provision. They seek Him for their own benefit; their service is self-motivated, not love-motivated.

Jesus said, "I never knew you." In this phrase the English word *knew* is a translation of the Greek word *ginosko*. In the New Testament it is used to describe intercourse between a man and a woman (Matt. 1:25). It represents intimacy. Jesus will say, "I never intimately knew you."

First Corinthians 8:3 says, "But if anyone loves God, this one is known by Him." In this case the word *known* uses the same Greek word *ginosko*. God intimately knows those who love Him. They have laid their lives down for Him (John 15:13). Only those who do this can keep His word. Remember, "He who does not love Me does not keep My words" (John 14:24). The true evidence of love for Jesus is not what is said but what is lived. No matter how passionately or boldly they say otherwise, those who are not submitted to God's authority do not love him. They know God, but God does not intimately know them.

Judas joined himself with Jesus. It appeared he loved Him. He dropped everything to follow Him. Judas stayed under the heat of persecution and the threat of death. He didn't quit when the other disciples did (John 6:66). He cast out devils, healed the sick, and preached the gospel. Jesus "called His twelve disciples [including Judas] together and gave them power and authority over all demons, and to cure diseases. He sent them to preach the kingdom of God and to heal the sick" (Luke 9:1–2).

However, Judas's motive was not right from the start. He never repented of his self-seeking ways. He revealed his true character when he went to the chief priests and said, "What are you willing to give me if I deliver Him to you?" (Matt. 26:14). He lied and flattered to gain advantage (Matt. 26:25). Throughout his time with Jesus he took money from the treasury of Jesus' ministry for personal use (John 12:4–6). He never knew Jesus intimately even though he spent three and a half years in His company!

Many today are like Judas. They have made sacrifices for the ministry, preached the gospel, and possibly even operated in the gifts yet have never intimately known Jesus. All their labor was stimulated by self-serving motives.

> But why do you call Me "Lord, Lord," and not do the things which I say?
>
> —LUKE 6:46

LIVE THE LIFE YOU CONFESS

The reference to *Lord* in the above verse originates from the Greek word *kurios*. Strong's dictionary of Greek words defines it as "supreme in authority or master." Jesus meant that there would be those who confess Him as Lord but do not follow Him as their supreme authority.

They live in a manner that does not support what they confess. They obey the will of God as long as it does not conflict with the desires of their own heart. If the will of God takes them in a different direction than the one they desire, they choose their own path yet still call Jesus "Lord."

Often success in ministry is measured purely by numbers. This mentality has caused many to do whatever was necessary to fill their altars with "converts" and their churches with "members." To accomplish this they preach Jesus as Savior but not as Lord. Their underlying message is, "Come to Jesus and get... salvation, peace, love, joy, prosperity, success, health, and so on." Yes, Jesus is the fulfillment of all these promises, but the benefits have been so overemphasized that the purity of the gospel has been reduced to a "now" answer to life's problems, followed with a lifetime guarantee of heaven.

This type of preaching merely entices sinners. They hear a watered-down message without hearing about repentance. "Give God a chance, and He will give you love, peace, and joy!" We bypass repentance in order to gain a "convert." So converts we have. But what kind?

Jesus confronted the ministers of His day: "You travel over land and sea to win a single convert, and when he becomes one, you make him twice as much a son of hell as you are" (Matt. 23:15, NIV). Converts are easily made, but are they truly obedient sons of the kingdom of God? These self-seeking converts are spawned by not only the message we have preached but also the one we have lived.

Jesus made it clear to the multitude, "Whoever desires to come after Me, let him deny himself, and take up his cross, and follow Me. For whoever desires to save his life will lose it, but whoever loses his life for My sake and the gospel's will save it" (Mark 8:34–35). If you isolate the word *desire* in this verse, you will notice that a desire to save your life will result in your losing it. Also note that when Jesus went on to talk about losing your life, He did not say, "Whoever *desires* to lose his life for My sake." Just desiring to lose your life is not enough—you must actually lose it!

The rich young ruler had an intense desire to be saved. He ran to Jesus and knelt before Him, crying out for eternal life. Yet his intense desire was not enough, for Jesus said to him, "You lack something." (See Mark 10:17–22.) He walked away when he realized the price of obedience. At least his honesty is to be respected!

There are thousands who do not attend church who would gladly receive the benefits of salvation if only they could keep the control of their own lives. Somehow they seem to realize what many in the church have missed: there is a price you pay to serve God. They are honest with God. They don't want to pay it. On the other hand, there are those who are deceived. They attend church, call Jesus "Lord," and declare their submission to His lordship, while in reality they are not in submission to the authority of God.

TWO DIFFERENT MESSAGES

I hope you now see the difference between the grace Jesus preached and the grace too many have believed. The present-day message of grace often extols, "Believe in Jesus; pray the sinner's prayer; confess Him as your Savior; and then you will enter the kingdom of heaven." There is very little mentioned about the cross or repentance.

Those who are converted in this manner tend to believe any disobedience is covered by the carte blanche grace of God. Could this condition be the reason for the lack of true spiritual authority and power in our churches?

I hope you hear this message in the spirit with which it has been delivered. I love God's people and desire them to prosper as their souls prosper. Therefore I am compelled to proclaim His truth. Teaching and doctrine shape an individual's beliefs and life. My heart breaks for the multitudes in churches who have been lulled into a lukewarm state. Paul instructed Timothy, "Watch your life and doctrine closely. Persevere in them, because if you do, you will save both yourself and your hearers" (1 Tim. 4:16, NIV). We must heed this warning. Perverted truth may sound good and may even appeal to our sense of reason, but it will lead to deception.

The truth of God's Word will feed you and build you up. It will also train you to discern between correct and incorrect thinking. Perverted truth can disqualify you for the kingdom. This is why God admonishes us to give His Word our full attention that we might correctly handle it. This chapter bears both warning and encouragement. The warning: don't allow incorrect doctrines of grace to disqualify you. The encouragement: there is the strength to live an obedient life through the grace of God that never fails. May the grace of our Lord Jesus Christ be with you.

9

THE FIGHT OF FAITH

DISOBEDIENCE IS CONTAGIOUS.

HAVE YOU EVER seen a person start their walk on fire for Jesus, only to end up in a lukewarm state after a process of time? You wonder, *How could someone so enthusiastic end up so lethargic in their walk?*

These people are the casualties of a battle they failed to recognize. Jude wrote a letter devoted entirely to addressing this conflict.

> Beloved, while I was very diligent to write to you concerning
>
> our common salvation, I found it necessary to write to you

exhorting you to contend earnestly for the faith which was once for all delivered to the saints.

—JUDE 3

Can you sense the urgency of the message? It is one of great importance. The Amplified Bible magnifies this further, "Beloved, my whole concern was to write to you in regard to our common salvation. [But] I found it necessary and was impelled to write you and urgently appeal to and exhort [you] to contend for the faith."

To contend is to battle or combat. The word *earnestly* indicates serious intent. We must ask this question, With what or with whom do we fight? I have heard different answers to this question. One suggests that we battle for the faith by speaking of our resistance toward demons in the heavenlies. Though this is valid spiritual warfare (see Ephesians 6:10–12), it is not the fight of which Jude is speaking. We can find the answer in the next statement in his letter.

For certain men have crept in unnoticed, who long ago were marked out for this condemnation, ungodly men, who turn the grace of our God into lewdness...

—JUDE 4

We must battle for the faith because certain individuals have slipped into our churches misrepresenting the grace of God as a cover-up or even license for sin. The Greek word for *lewdness* is *aselgeia*. Strong's dictionary of Greek New Testament words defines this as "lasciviousness, unbridled lust or excess." These individuals pervert the grace of God by living excessive, fleshly lifestyles while proclaiming their salvation by grace. The Living Bible sheds further light on this. It declares these people show "that after we become Christians we can do just as we like without fear of God's punishment" (Jude 4).

Jude said these men also "deny the only Lord God and our Lord Jesus Christ" (Jude 4). Some of you may be thinking, *No one could come into our churches today and speak out a denial of God and our Lord Jesus Christ.* You're right—anyone who tried to do that couldn't get away with it anymore today than they could in Jude's day. But Jude indicated these people *creep in unnoticed.* No one who openly denies Jesus as the Christ could remain unnoticed. The following verse sheds some light on how these people manage to creep in:

> To the pure, all things are pure, but to those who are corrupted and do not believe, nothing is pure. In fact, both their minds and consciences are corrupted. They claim to know God, but by their actions they deny Him.
>
> —TITUS 1:15–16, NIV

They do not deny the Lord by what they say but do so by their lifestyles or actions. At the same time they believe they know the Lord! Paul called such people impostors.

> But wicked men and imposters will go on from bad to worse, deceiving and leading astray others and being deceived and led astray themselves.
>
> —2 TIMOTHY 3:13, AMP

An impostor is one who deceives others by an assumed character or false pretense (like the wolf in sheep's clothing). Paul did not limit their deception to others—he said their influence extended to their own selves. They really believe they serve the Lord. They confess a new birth experience, speaking fluently in the language of the Scriptures as they participate in Christian activities. The only way to discern them is by the fruit of their lives (Matt. 7:18–20).

These imposters "defile the flesh, reject authority, and speak evil of dignitaries" (Jude 8). They are "grumblers, complainers, walking according to their own lusts [desires]; and they mouth great swelling words, flattering people to gain advantage...These are sensual [worldly minded] persons, who cause divisions" (Jude 16, 19). Is this not an accurate description of many who create problems in homes, ministries, and churches? Many naive, innocent people have been influenced by their behavior.

> Woe to them! For they have gone in the way of Cain, have run
> greedily in the error of Balaam for profit, and perished in the
> rebellion of Korah.
>
> —JUDE 11

He compares these people with three men of the Old Testament—
Cain, Balaam, and Korah, all who at one time enjoyed fellowship
with God or were in the service of God.

Cain presented a disobedient offering, became offended, rebelled
against the counsel of God, and committed a murder.

Balaam was greedy for power, position, and money, and he pros-
tituted the anointing on his life. Because of this, Balaam died by the
edge of the sword at God's command (Josh. 13:22).

Korah was a priest and a descendant of Levi, yet he rose up in
opposition to Moses and Aaron in the wilderness, claiming, "You
take too much upon yourselves...Why then do you exalt yourselves
above the assembly of the LORD?" (Num. 16:3). His concern was not
that Moses was overburdened; he wanted a share of Moses' authority.
His hidden agenda was to promote himself. Insubordinate to God's
appointed leadership, he accused Moses (whom God had exalted)
of exalting himself. By doing this, Korah set himself against God's
authority (Rom. 13:1–2). His rebellion was judged when he was swal-
lowed alive by the earth (Num. 16:31–33).

Cain, Balaam, and Korah were unable to maintain their relation-
ships with God because their goal was to serve themselves. It was not
the service of God or His people they sought. Jude described these
people further by saying:

> These are spots in your love feasts, while they feast with you
> without fear, serving only themselves.
>
> —JUDE 12

Love feasts were common meals eaten together by the early
church.[1] Any sort of Christian gathering today could represent a love
feast. The imposters who attended these feasts were called "spots"

because of their conduct. Jesus is coming back for a "glorious church, not having spot of wrinkle or any such thing" (Eph. 5:27). Imposters will not be found in the assembly of the righteous on the Day of the Lord. Jude continues:

> They are clouds without water, carried about by the winds.
>
> —Jude 12

Clouds without water illustrate the emptiness of their condition. Though they bear a semblance of godliness, they are void of the character of Jesus. They have the appearance of a believer without the life or substance of one. Take a careful look at the next statement made concerning these people.

> Late autumn trees without fruit, twice dead, pulled up by the roots.
>
> —Jude 12

Jude compares them to late autumn trees with no fruit. Autumn is the time of harvest when fruit should be fully ripe and hanging on the tree. He described these barren, uprooted trees as "twice dead." What a description—twice dead! In order to be twice dead you would have to be once dead, be made alive, and then die again. This describes people who were dead without Christ, then received salvation only to die again because they permanently departed from Him in their hearts.

ONCE SAVED ALWAYS SAVED?

A very deceptive doctrine has been propagated throughout the church. It claims that once an individual is saved there is no way they can ever lose their salvation. It is a controversial subject, yet it need not be. The only reason it is controversial is because some teachings have twisted the Scriptures until they say what we want to hear as opposed to God's truth. If a person's heart is set on an issue, they will funnel all Scripture through what they believe rather than believe what they read.

I challenge you to examine what the Bible has to say about it. Don't filter these scriptures through the teaching of Dr. So-and-So, but compare verse to verse and hear what the Spirit of God is saying. Listen with your heart; it will not lie to you. There is no reason to fear truth if you love God. For if you truly love Him, you will never want to leave Him!

We first need to determine which verses refer to individuals who have been saved. There is a good example in James.

> Brethren, if anyone among you wanders from the truth, and someone turns him back, let him know that he who turns a sinner from the error of his way will save a soul from death and cover a multitude of sins.
>
> —James 5:19–20

Notice James said "brethren" and "if anyone among you." He was not addressing those who just think they are Christians; he was describing a believer who had wandered from the way of truth. Again note that James called a brother who wandered from the truth a sinner. If they are not turned back by repentance, their destination is death. Jude described them as "twice dead." It is obvious from James these people were once alive in Jesus. The Book of Proverbs amplifies this point.

> A man who wanders from the way of understanding will rest in the assembly of the dead.
>
> —Proverbs 21:16

In order to wander from the truth you must first walk in it. But once a person wanders from the truth, if he or she does not return to the path of righteousness, their final destination will be "the assembly of the dead," which is hell. Peter wrote:

> For if, after they have escaped the pollutions of the world through the knowledge of the Lord and Savior Jesus Christ...
>
> —2 Peter 2:20

Before we go on, ask yourself, Would a person who has escaped the pollution of this world by the knowledge of the Lord Jesus Christ be saved? Without a doubt you should answer yes. So Peter is talking about people who have been saved. Now let's continue:

> ...they are again entangled in them and overcome, the latter end is worse for them than the beginning. For it would have been better for them not to have known the way of righteousness, than having known it, to turn from the holy commandment delivered to them.
>
> —2 Peter 2:20–21

These people returned to the world, were overcome by its power, and did not seek to restore their relationship to the Lord. Backsliders can return to the Lord through genuine repentance (we just read that in James). But if they stay entangled it would have been better for them never to have known the way of righteousness. In other words, in God's eyes it is better never to have been saved than to receive the gift of eternal life and turn from it permanently.

How could it be better to have never known the way of righteousness? Jude answers this by saying they are "twice dead...for whom is reserved the blackness of darkness forever" (Jude 12–13).

An eternity of blackest darkness is reserved for them. Those who received Jesus, knew His will, and still walked permanently away will receive the greatest punishment of the second death. (See Revelation 2:11; 20:6, 14; 21:8.) Jesus described their torment.

> But if that servant says in his heart, "My master [He is a servant and calls the Lord his master] is delaying his coming," and begins to beat the male and female servants, and to eat and drink and be drunk [a self-seeking life], the master of that servant will come on a day when he is not looking for him, and at an hour when he is not aware, and will cut him in two and appoint him his portion with the unbelievers. [Notice his final resting place will be with the assembly of the unbelievers or the

dead.] And that servant who knew his master's will, and did not prepare himself or do according to his will, *shall be beaten with many stripes* [the more severe punishment]. But he who did not know, yet committed things deserving of stripes, shall be beaten with few.

—LUKE 12:45–48, EMPHASIS ADDED

I NEVER KNEW YOU

In the last chapter we saw the first group of individuals who will expect to hear Jesus say enter into heaven but instead will hear Him say, "I never knew you; depart from Me you who practice lawlessness!" (Matt. 7:23). It is made up of people who join themselves to Jesus solely for the benefits of salvation. These people follow Jesus at first, but their lack of commitment is ultimately revealed (as in Judas Iscariot).

Now we meet the second group of people from Matthew 7:22–23. (See page 105.) These are those who lose their salvation, the ones who at one time knew Him and even did wonders in His name yet did not endure to the end. Jesus also rebuked these people with "I never knew you." How could this be?

> But when a righteous man turns away from his righteousness and commits iniquity, and does according to all the abominations that the wicked man does, shall he live? All the righteousness which he has done shall not be remembered; because of the unfaithfulness of which he is guilty and the sin which he has committed, because of them he shall die.
>
> —EZEKIEL 18:24

God said He would not remember their righteousness. It would be as if it had never happened. This means He will forget it ever existed. It is as if He never knew this person. This is the reason Jesus will say to those who do not endure to the end, "I never knew you."

He will forget their righteousness just as surely as He will forgive and forget the sins of the righteous. He says, "This is the covenant that

I will make with them after those days, saith the Lord, I will put my laws into their hearts, and in their minds will I write them; And their sins and iniquities will I remember no more" (Heb. 10:16–17, KJV). God refuses to remember our sins. The devil will, and he accuses us. But God declares, "I have no remembrance of the sins you accuse them of!" In the eyes of God it is as though we have never sinned.

JUDE'S MAIN POINT

Let's summarize what Jude wanted to say. He urged us to fight earnestly for the faith and described the focus and nature of our battle. The focus is upon those who say they are Christians but only obey God if it is convenient to their self-ruled life. Either they have never been believers, as in the case of Judas, or they have fallen from grace. Whichever the case, they are lukewarm impostors, false brethren, wolves in sheep's clothing, and spots in the church.

Virtually every voice of the New Testament—Jesus, Paul, Peter, Jude, and the apostle John—warned of those who would fall away. Likewise, I have joined my voice to their warning. Why? It is the voice of love spoken for the sake of protection! In this we discover the nature of our battle: to keep ourselves and those under our care from falling into the same state as these in disobedience.

After Jude warned of those who would pervert the grace of God, he gave us this strong exhortation of protection:

> But you, beloved, building yourselves up on your most holy faith, praying in the Holy Spirit, keep yourselves in the love of God.
>
> —JUDE 20–21

We are to keep ourselves in the love of God. Remember, those who love God are obedient to Him (John 14:15). Jude warns of the leaven of disobedience filtering into your life. (See 1 Corinthians 5:6.) Disobedience is contagious. If you hang around a person with a contagious illness, your own resistance will eventually be worn down, and you will fall prey to it. It is the same with disobedience, but God's words of warning and instruction are like immunization shots. They boost our immunity and resistance to the virus of disobedience.

Suppose a very contagious disease was spreading throughout your community, but there was also an antidote to prevent the contraction of the disease. Would you immunize your children and teach them preventative health care? Yes, absolutely! We would afford them the protection of the antidote and educate them to prevent the spread of the disease.

Even so the Lord and those who penned His Word have gone to great lengths to warn us of the contagious diseases of lukewarmness and disobedience. Listen to the warning given to the elders of Asia:

> Therefore take heed to yourselves and to all the flock, among which the Holy Spirit has made you overseers, to shepherd the church of God which He purchased with His own blood. For I know this, that after my departure savage wolves will come in among you, not sparing the flock. Also from among your-selves men will rise up, speaking perverse things, to draw away the disciples after themselves. Therefore watch, and remember that for three years I did not cease to warn everyone night and day with tears.
>
> —ACTS 20:28–31

Hear his words, "take heed." It is a warning he repeated night and day, pleading with tears for three years. He wanted to keep his spiritual children from the disease of disobedience. He said that wolves would come in among them. Jesus likened false prophets who come into the church to wolves dressed in sheep's clothing (Matt. 7:15). They talk like Christians but can be discerned by their fruit (Matt. 7:16). Wolves easily enter a flock when the shepherd is not protecting them.

Often we want to hear only encouraging and positive messages. However, Paul made it clear that to fully preach the gospel we must *warn* as well as *encourage*. By doing this we will present every man perfect in Christ Jesus (Col. 1:28). Understanding and obeying the

Bible's warnings from God are key elements in the completion of our journey in Christ.

David realized the value of God's precepts. He described them:

> The judgments of the LORD are true and righteous altogether.
> More to be desired are they than gold,
> Yea, than much fine gold;
> Sweeter also than honey and the honeycomb.
> Moreover by them Your servant is warned,
> And in keeping them there is great reward.
>
> —PSALM 19:9–11

To the mature believer the entire counsel of God's Word is sweet, including His warnings. There is a great reward to those who heed them.

Ministers are called not only to feed God's sheep but also to protect them. They are to warn of the snares of the enemy. Many ministers have withdrawn from warning their people because they think it is a negative message. It is not negative but preventive—it saves lives and churches!

Jesus is certainly not negative, yet He said, "Take heed that no one deceives you" (Matt. 24:4). Again He charged His disciples, "Take heed, beware of the leaven of the Pharisees and the leaven of Herod" (Mark 8:15). The contagious leaven of the Pharisees was legalism, which leads to hypocrisy. The contagious leaven of Herod was a disobedient, fleshly lifestyle, which also leads to hypocrisy. These are two contagious diseases that can attack an unaware person and lead them into a disobedient lifestyle.

Peter warned us with, "You therefore, beloved, since you know this beforehand, beware lest you also fall from your own steadfastness, being led away with the error of the wicked" (2 Pet. 3:17). Hear what he is saying. When a person is not warned, he can easily fall away from his steadfast obedience by the error of those who have already fallen.

ENEMY ACCESS DENIED

LUKEWARM BREEDING GROUNDS

Some of the most difficult places at which to minister are established Christian organizations. Christian schools seem to top the list. I could write chapters on numerous experiences I've had in them. I won't because this is not the purpose of this book.

These institutions are hard to reach because they are lukewarm breeding grounds for rebellion and disobedience. It may start with a handful of students, often the most established. These young people have grown up in Sunday school and youth group and confess a born-again experience. Yet they are disrespectful to authority, bound by lust, and some have even experimented with drugs or alcohol at a young age. They are obsessed with professional sports figures, Hollywood, dating, and other worldly pursuits. Often they are the sons and daughters of the church leaders, yet they were not trained as children to discern compromise and hypocrisy. This makes them all the more callous and dangerous.

These hardened students seem unaware that their lifestyles preach a message to those around them. (What we live preaches louder than what we speak.) The message: you can be saved and still serve yourself and love the world.

This confuses the other students and new converts. Bewildered they ask, "How can Christians live like this?" At first they are shocked. Then reasoning sets in, and they conclude that God doesn't really care how they live. Rebellion is all right. The doctrine of perverted grace begins to permeate their thinking, encouraged by the lascivious lifestyle of their fellow students. There is more pressure to conform to the disobedience than to maintain a standard of godliness. Paul explained this dilemma.

> Don't you realize that if even one person is allowed to go on sinning, soon all will be affected?
>
> —1 CORINTHIANS 5:6, TLB

One particular Christian high school comes to mind. It was known as one of the finest college preparatory schools in the state.

They took pride in the individual Christian character of the students. Most of the students came from Christian homes and were well-churched.

They had a chapel service once a week that lasted a punctual fifty minutes. It was reported to me that the principal had been known to take the microphone from ministers who exceeded their allotted time. When I came to address this chapel, I was met with rolling eyes, glares of defiance, and slouched and slumbering bodies. I sensed an extreme hardness of heart in the students. Their aloof attitudes and obstinence sent a clear message to me: "We've heard it all before. Hurry up, and get this over with!" It brought to mind God's word to Ezekiel.

> The whole house of Israel is hardened and obstinate. But I will make you as unyielding and hardened as they are. I will make your forehead like the hardest stone, harder than flint. Do not be afraid of them or terrified by them, though they are a rebellious house.
>
> —Ezekiel 3:7–9, niv

I have learned that the prophetic anointing of God will arise stronger in the face of hardened people. The harder the people, the stronger the prophetic message. Yet it is for the sake of love and restoration, not for punishment. It often takes a good blow from a sledge hammer to crack a hardened heart. God says, "Is not My word...like a hammer that breaks the rock in pieces?" (Jer. 23:29).

As I preached I sensed the prophetic anointing increasing. I proclaimed many of the truths you've read in the last two chapters. The students' posture began to change. Now instead of withdrawing from me, they leaned forward. They appeared somewhat startled as they fixed their eyes on me. The light of God's word pierced their hearts and exposed their disobedience. It was as if they were waking from a dream, jarred by the realization of the contamination of their hearts. As they saw it for what it was, it became more than they could bear. Conviction gripped them as many realized that although they'd been raised in Christian homes, they had never been truly saved, or they had backslidden. By the time I was finished speaking, tears brimmed in their eyes and shone upon their cheeks.

The altar call was simple, "Those of you who have not completely given your life to Jesus as Master come down to the front." Of the 230 students present, 185 rushed forward! Girls had streaks of mascara running down their school uniforms as their tears flowed.

The chapel should have been dismissed by 9:35 a.m. I gave the altar call at 9:25, yet the students stayed in the chapel under the power of the Holy Spirit until 11:30 a.m. Their hardness was broken before a holy God! Hallelujah!

God had moved on the principal, and he pleaded with me, "John, we have been praying for this. Please come back tomorrow morning. We will postpone all classes and arrange a special chapel service so you can speak again."

I agreed.

When I relayed all this to the pastor who had coordinated the chapel service, he could not believe his ears. He knew how rigid the school schedule was. I explained how the word of God had torn down those tough walls. In the past most of the ministers who had spoken at the chapel services of this school had tried to win the acceptance of the students rather than boldly proclaiming truth.

The following day chapel began promptly at 8:45 a.m. I told the principal I would try and finish by 9:35 a.m. He encouraged me, "Please do whatever needs to be done, and don't be concerned with the time." This time the student assembly was hungry and attentive. A few wept as they testified of the impact the previous service had on their lives. When I rose to preach, the prophetic anointing was strong. Again I warned of the contamination of disobedience, reminding them that rock is not ground into dust with a single blow.

This day the majority of the students who had not responded on the first day came forward at the close of this service. The students who had repented at the altar only the day before came with them, this time addressing other areas of their lives. Once again the Spirit of God fell as the students wept in repentance. That chapel did not dismiss until 11:15 a.m.!

Our family was in the San Diego airport a year later, some fifteen hundred miles from where these chapel services had taken place. While we watched the carousel for our luggage a young man approached me. With the utmost respect, he introduced himself and shared that he had been in those two chapels the previous year. He said his life had been profoundly changed by that encounter with a holy God. I sensed his regard for the uncompromising word God had revealed to him in those chapel services. My heart swelled with joy as it recognized the evidence of a changed life. To God be the glory!

I could tell many such stories. They are not limited to Christian schools but extend to numerous churches and Bible colleges. I have preached in services where hundreds of people began to weep before a holy God. Their tears brought a cleansing they had not experienced previously. They left the service not under the law or condemnation but with an awesome awareness of the love, mercy, and grace of God.

I've had businessmen come to me with tears in their eyes, thanking me for obeying God. I've heard it over and over, "John, I was in a lukewarm state and would have been vomited out of Jesus' mouth had He not brought His word to me today." I have listened to this same testimony from people from all walks of life. The most wonderful part is that these testimonies endure! Years later I hear from individuals or from their pastors telling me they still burn in their obedience to the Lord.

Jesus is not coming back for a lukewarm bride who fornicates with the world. He is coming for a consecrated bride, unspotted by the world. Would you marry someone who said, "I'll be faithful to you for 364 days a year, but give me one day a year to jump in bed with my old lovers"? Of course not! Neither would Jesus. He is not coming for a bride who has reserved a portion of her heart for the world! Don't be deceived. Don't be contaminated. Don't be infected by the subtlety of disobedience. Do not stray from your steadfast post to be led away to a lukewarm cesspool.

ENEMY ACCESS DENIED

At the close of this chapter I challenge you to read the Bible in the light of what the Spirit of God has revealed to you through these last two chapters. I realize this message may not have lifted you to a new dimension of happiness, but it holds a wealth of understanding and wisdom that will guard your eternal joy at the possible expense of your temporary happiness. May the grace of our Lord be with you.

10

HUMILITY—THE ROAD TO SUCCESS

A PROUD PERSON
BLAMES EVERYONE WHILE
EXCUSING HIMSELF.

A PERSON IS THE most susceptible to falling when he is doing well. When he reaches a level of success, it is easy to forget the grace that transported him there. Because this is true, we are to "be clothed with humility, for God resists the proud, but gives grace to the humble" (1 Pet. 5:5).

REMAIN HUMBLE OR BE HUMBLED

Uzziah, a descendant of King David, was crowned king at the age of sixteen. At first he sought God diligently. You would too if you were made ruler of a nation at age sixteen. More than likely he was over-whelmed and humbled by the magnitude of the undertaking. Yet "as long as he sought the LORD, God made him prosper" (2 Chron. 26:5).

Because he utterly relied on God, he was greatly blessed. He made war against the Philistines, defeating them in numerous cities, as well as the Arabians, Meunites, and Ammonites. Under his lead the nation become strong both economically and militarily. There was an abundance of prosperity under his leadership. All this success was the result of the grace of God on his life. But over time something changed: his humility was replaced by his own confidence.

> But when he was strong his heart was lifted up, to his destruc-tion, for he transgressed against the LORD his God by entering the temple of the LORD to burn incense on the altar of incense.
> —2 CHRONICLES 26:16

It was not in a weak moment, but when Uzziah was strong, that his heart was lifted in pride. As he surveyed the prosperity and suc-cess that encompassed all his domain his heart ceased to seek the Lord. He could do it on his own now; he knew how. As his achieve-ments mounted, he assumed God would continue to bless all he undertook just as God had done when he humbly sought Him.

His rise to pride did not happen overnight. But it can easily happen to anyone. God warned me, "John, most people in the kingdom who have fallen have not done so in the dry times, but in the times of abundance."

This is a pattern many Christians fall into. When they are first saved, they hunger to know the Lord and His ways. Their humility is evident because they seek Him and trust Him for everything. They arrive at church with a hunger in their hearts, "Lord, I want to know You!" They submit to God's direct and delegated authority. But after they have amassed knowledge and waxed strong through experience, their attitudes change.

Now, instead of reading their Bible with the intent of, "Lord, reveal Yourself and Your ways to me," they use it to support their established doctrine, reading what they believe instead of believing what they read. No longer do they listen for God's heavenly voice in the voice of their pastor. Instead they fold their arms and lean back with the attitude, "I'll see what he knows." They are experts in Scriptures but have forfeited their tenderness and humility of heart. The grace to serve God now wanes.

First Corinthians 8:1 says, "We know that we all have knowledge. Knowledge puffs up [pride], but love edifies." Love does not seek its own but lays its life down for the Master and those it is called to serve. Pride seeks its own behind a mask of religion. God explained that knowledge gained without love results in pride.

TWO FORCES THAT STRENGTHEN EACH OTHER

When pride entered the heart of King Uzziah, did he become more or less religious? The amazing answer: he became more religious! His heart was lifted up, and he entered the temple to perform his so-called worship. Pride and a religious spirit go hand in hand. A religious spirit causes a person to think he is humble because of his appearance of spirituality. The truth is, he is proud. A proud person stays in bondage to a religious spirit because he is too proud to admit he has such a spirit! This is one reason pride is so well-camouflaged in the church. It hides behind a religious, charismatic, Pentecostal, or evangelical mask.

Azariah and the other eighty priests of the temple went into the sanctuary where Uzziah was burning incense and confronted him, saying, "It is not for you, Uzziah, to burn incense to the LORD . . . Get out of the sanctuary for you have trespassed! You shall have no honor from the LORD God (2 Chron. 26:18). Watch Uzziah's response when confronted by the priests.

> Then Uzziah became furious; and he had a censer in his hand to burn incense. And while he was angry with the priests, leprosy broke out on his forehead, before the priests in the house of the LORD, beside the incense altar.
>
> —2 CHRONICLES 26:19

Uzziah became angry. Pride will always justify itself. This self-defense will be coupled with anger. A proud person blames everyone else while excusing himself. Uzziah directed his anger at the priests, but the problem lay deep within his own bosom. Pride had blinded his eyes! Instead of humbling himself, he allowed anger to fuel his pride. Leprosy broke out on his forehead where all could see it. In this case, leprosy was an outward manifestation of an inward condition.

Leprosy in the Old Testament is a type of sin in the New Testament. It is a sad but true commentary that many mighty people have fallen into sin in the church. One example is sexual sin. God spoke to me, "John, with many of these who fall into sin, the root is not the sin itself, but the root is pride."

Our Most Deadly Foe

Pride is a subtle and deadly foe yet so easily camouflaged. Those in pride are ignorant of their true condition. Only humility can expose it. Pride is the very root of rebellion, and we see its influence right from the start—when Lucifer rebelled against God. God described Lucifer's heart condition.

> You were the anointed cherub who covers;
> I established you;
> You were on the holy mountain of God;
> You walked back and forth in the midst of fiery stones.
> You were perfect in your ways from the day you were created,
> Till iniquity was found in you.
>
> By the abundance of your trading
> You became filled with violence within,
> And you sinned...
>
> Your heart was lifted up because of your beauty;
> You corrupted your wisdom for the sake of your splendor.
> —Ezekiel 28:14–17

All that he was and all that he possessed were a gift from God. Yet at some point he forgot this and longed for more. His heart became lifted up, and he wished to enforce his will. Issuing forth from the pride in his heart he made several proclamations, all which begin with the words, "I will" (Isa. 14:12–15). There was no humility within him. He was cast out of God's presence.

Hear this, servant of the Lord. God gives grace to the humble while resisting the proud. You never find the grace of God in an individual who has forgotten where he came from and the One who brought him out. James said:

> But He gives more grace. Therefore He says: "God resists the proud, but gives grace to the humble." Therefore submit to God. Resist the devil and he will flee from you.
>
> —James 4:6–7

We resist the devil by our submission to God. Our humility and obedience usher in God's grace, which is a mighty weapon against the evil one.

GRACE THAT REDEEMS

Though we discussed grace thoroughly in chapter eight, I want to remind you again of grace's function in the believer's life.

We are told of Jesus:

> For we do not have a High Priest who cannot sympathize with our weaknesses, but was in all points tempted as we are, yet without sin. Let us therefore come boldly to the throne of grace, that we may obtain mercy and find grace to help in time of need.
>
> —Hebrews 4:15–16

He gives us mercy and grace in order to help us. He is merciful toward our ignorance and weakness (1 Tim. 1:13; Heb. 5:2) but not

135

toward willful disobedience (Heb. 10:26–31). He supplies the grace necessary to overcome our weakness.

In this light we have a new understanding of the truth: "My grace is sufficient for you, for My strength is made perfect in weakness" (2 Cor. 12:9). Our weakness is our inability to obey God in our own strength. It is not possible to live the life God expects of us on our own. But He adds His strength to our weakness. This aid is called grace. So we can say grace gives us the ability to fulfill what truth demands. This is confirmed by Hebrews 12:28, "Therefore, since we are receiving a kingdom which cannot be shaken, let us have grace, by which we may serve God acceptably."

Receiving God's grace is not a onetime experience. James told believers, "But He gives us more and more grace" (James 4:6, AMP). We need it every moment of every day. In each epistle Paul begins with greetings of, "Grace to you from God our Father and the Lord Jesus Christ." These letters were for believers, illustrating our continual need for God's grace.

We are also encouraged to grow in the grace of God (2 Pet. 3:17–18). As we do our hearts are strengthened to fulfill God's will and shun the will of man. We see this exemplified in the life of Jesus: "And the Child grew and became strong in spirit, filled with wisdom; and the grace of God was upon Him" (Luke 2:40). The grace of God on His life empowered Him to develop a strong spirit and fulfill the will of His Father.

There are various degrees of grace. This is revealed in Acts 4:33, "And with great power the apostles gave witness to the resurrection of the Lord Jesus. And great grace was upon them all." We should hunger for greater degrees of God's grace. The greater the grace, the greater our capacity to serve and glorify the Lord. And remember, God's Word says the pathway to grace is humility.

A LIFE THAT EXEMPLIFIES HUMILITY

We are to walk continually in humility, for God gives His grace only to those who are of a contrite spirit (James 4:6–7), those who are utterly dependent upon Him. We see this humility or complete dependence upon God's grace in Paul.

> Now I am glad to boast about how weak I am; I am glad to be a living demonstration of Christ's power, instead of showing off my own power and abilities...for when I am weak, then I am strong—the less I have, the more I depend on him.
> —2 CORINTHIANS 12:9–10, TLB

Hear his words, "The less I have, the more I depend on him." This was the progression of Paul's life. As you study it, you will find that the longer he lived, the more dependent on God's grace he became and the less he relied on his own strength. This attitude breeds humility. The longer Paul lived, the more he emptied himself for the sake of Christ.

When he was first saved, Paul humbled himself by forsaking all he had achieved in the flesh, laying aside all his accomplishments as nothing but vanity.

> But all these things that I once thought very worthwhile—now I've thrown them all away so that I can put my trust and hope in Christ alone.
> —PHILIPPIANS 3:7, TLB

All who come to Jesus and are genuinely born again reach this place. However, humility does not stop there; it is progressive.

Proceeding with Paul as an example, he was a leader with an abundance of spiritual revelation and wisdom. This afforded him the opportunity to achieve much in his service to the Lord. But his knowledge easily could have become a stumbling block. He willingly released all he had achieved before his conversion, but what about after he became a Christian leader? Would he allow wisdom and accomplishment to lift his heart, or would he continue to depend upon God's grace? We find the answer in Paul's own words written after years of successful ministry.

> For I am the least of the apostles, who am not worthy to be
> called an apostle, because I persecuted the church of God.
>
> —1 Corinthians 15:9

Do you hear the humility in these words? He did not even consider himself worthy to be called an apostle because of the terrible things he did prior to his conversion. Yet this man received possibly the greatest revelation truth of God's forgiveness—that a man in Christ Jesus is a new creation. Previous moral and spiritual conditions have passed away, and all things have become new (2 Cor. 5:17). Even with this revelation and the accompanying ministry exploits, he still remembered the magnitude and greatness of God's mercy toward him.

> But by the grace of God I am what I am, and His grace toward
> me was not in vain; but I labored more abundantly than they
> all, yet not I, but the grace of God which was with me.
>
> —1 Corinthians 15:10

"I labored more abundantly than all the other apostles"! Is Paul talking out of both sides of his mouth? This comment sounds arrogant, yet it is not. It precedes another declaration of Paul's dependence on God. He followed his assessment of himself as the least of the apostles with an acknowledgment that all he had done had only been by God's ability. He was fully aware that all he had achieved spiritually flowed from the unmerited favor and grace of God.

Paul wrote this letter to the Corinthians in A.D. 55.[1] His self-description as "the least of all the apostles" is hard to swallow. Both in his day and throughout the history of the church, Paul has been esteemed as one of the greatest apostles. Now consider what he said to the Ephesians seven years later in A.D. 62 after further ministry accomplishments.[2]

> I became a minister according to the gift of the grace of God
> given to me by the effective working of His power. To me, who

am less than the least of all the saints, this grace was given, that I should preach among the Gentiles the unsearchable riches of Christ.

—Ephesians 3:7–8

Seven years earlier he called himself the least apostle, and now he describes himself as lower than the least of all the saints! What? If anyone could boast in their Christianity, it surely was Paul. Yet the longer he served the Lord, the smaller he saw himself. His humility was progressive. Could this be why the grace of God on his life increased proportionately the older he became?

At the close of his life Paul sent two letters to Timothy.[3] Hear again how Paul described himself:

This is a faithful saying and worthy of all acceptance, that Christ Jesus came into the world to save sinners, of whom I am chief.

—1 Timothy 1:15

Now he is the "chief of sinners"! He did not say, "I *was* chief." He said, "I *am* chief." After years of great accomplishment, his confession was not, "I have done it all; my great ministry should be esteemed." Nor did he say, "I have done a great work and deserve the respect of a true apostle." It was not, "I am the least of the apostles," as he had written several years earlier, nor was it, "I am least of the saints." It was, "Of all sinners, I am chief." Though he knew that in Christ he was the righteousness of God (2 Cor. 5:21), he never lost sight of God's grace and mercy. In fact, the longer he lived, the more dependent he became on His grace.

This explains another statement Paul made toward the end of his life.[4]

Brethren, I do not count myself to have apprehended; but one thing I do, forgetting those things which are behind and reaching forward to those things which are ahead, I press toward

the goal for the prize of the upward call of God in Christ Jesus.
—PHILIPPIANS 3:13–14

Can you hear the humility in his words: "I haven't arrived, and what I have achieved, I leave behind in thought. It is nothing compared to the quest to fully know Christ Jesus my Lord"?

Notice he said, "I press toward the goal." To press means there is resistance and opposition. One of the greatest opponents to the upward call is pride. That's the reason the upward call is so easy to miss.

HUMBLING VERSUS DEFENDING OURSELVES

We believers need to battle against the foe of pride rather than battle for our rights or privileges. We waste so much time defending ourselves. This leads to factions and contention. One time my wife and I were having intense fellowship (quarreling). In the heat of it, the Lord spoke this to me: "Your pride is being exposed." I was immediately convicted as the following scripture rose up in my spirit:

By pride comes nothing but strife, but with the well-advised is wisdom.

—PROVERBS 13:10

God continued, "John, any time you and Lisa fight, you'll find pride lurking somewhere, and you must deal with it." But one may argue, "What if I know I'm right?" Allow Jesus to answer this question, "Agree with your adversary quickly" (Matt. 5:25). By refusing to defend yourself, one if not both of the following will happen. First, you lay down pride, which will open your eyes to recognize flaws in your own character that went previously undetected. Second, if you are right, you are still following the example of Christ by allowing God His rightful place as judge of the situation.

For this is commendable, if because of conscience toward God one endures grief, suffering wrongfully…For to this you were called, because Christ also suffered for us, leaving us an example, that you should follow His steps: "Who committed no sin, nor was deceit found in His mouth"; who, when He was reviled, did not revile in return; when He suffered, He did not threaten, but committed Himself to Him who judges righteously.

—1 PETER 2:19, 21–23

This is our calling: to follow Christ's example, who suffered when He was not at fault. This precept wars against the natural mind since its logic appears absurd. However, the wisdom of God proves that humility and obedience make room for God's righteous judgment. Defense, correction, vindication, or whatever other response is appropriate should proceed from the hand of God, not from man. An individual who vindicates himself does not walk in humility of Christ. No one on earth possesses more authority than Jesus, yet He never defended himself.

And while He was being accused by the chief priests and elders, He answered nothing. Then Pilate said to Him, "Do You not hear how many things they testify against You?" But He answered him not one word, so that the governor marveled greatly.

—MATTHEW 27:12–14

Jesus was accused of a complete lie! There was not a morsel of truth in what they accused Him of. Yet He did not correct his accusers or defend Himself. His behavior caused the governor to marvel at His composure. He had never seen such behavior from a man.

Why didn't Jesus defend Himself? It was so that He could remain under His Father's judgment and thus His protection. Remember Peter said, "When He was reviled, did not revile in return...but committed Himself to Him who judges righteously" (1 Pet. 2:23). When we refuse to defend ourselves we are hidden under the hand of God's grace and judgment. There is no safer place.

> Who shall bring a charge against God's elect? It is God who
> justifies.
>
> —ROMANS 8:33

In contrast, those who defend themselves come under the judgment of their accusers. The moment you justify or defend yourself before another you yield to them as your judge. You have forfeited your authority or position in Christ, for your accuser rises above you when you answer his criticism. Yes, his authority is elevated above you because of your self-defense. Attempting to prove your innocence, you succumb to the mercy of your accuser.

> Agree with your adversary quickly, while you are on the way
> with him, lest your adversary deliver you to the judge, the judge
> hand you over to the officer, and you be thrown into prison.
> Assuredly, I say to you, you will by no means get out of there till
> you have paid the last penny.
>
> —MATTHEW 5:25–26

According to this parable you will be made to pay whatever your accuser demands as restitution. You are left helpless and at his mercy. The greater the offense he bears toward you, the less mercy he will extend to you. He will exact every last penny of your debt.

Pride would say, "Defend yourself." Jesus said, "Agree with your adversary." In so doing you lay down pride and make God the judge of the situation.

THE EXAMPLE OF A CHILD'S HUMILITY

During the school year Addison, my nine-year-old son, told us about a problem he faced at school. He believed that one of his instructors disliked him and blamed him whenever there was talking or disorder in the class. This had gone on for a while, and now this teacher had sent home a note that was to be placed on record against him. Addison is extremely conscientious, and this was all too much for him to bear. As he shared his fears and frustration, he broke down in tears at our dinner table.

We assured him we would believe the best about him and asked him to relay the details as he could best remember them. He said, "I get blamed for everything that goes wrong. If there is more than one person to blame, I still receive all the blame. Not only that, I am blamed for things I haven't done. Today, the two boys next to me were laughing and giggling, and the teacher turned around and yelled at me." His lip began to quiver, and the tears began to well. To a nine-year-old, this was a hopeless crisis.

All Addison's other teachers had reported his conduct as excellent, so I knew this was an isolated situation. I asked him, "What did you say when the teacher blamed you?"

Addison quickly answered, "I told him, 'I wasn't talking. It was those two boys!'"

I asked, "Is this the way you usually respond when you're corrected by him?"

Addison replied, "Yes, if I know I wasn't doing anything."

I looked at him, "Well, son, this is where the problem lies. You are defending yourself. When you defend yourself, God will not."

I shared some scriptures with him. Then I shared a tough personal example of my own that he could relate to. I had worked on the staff of a large church. My immediate superior disliked me. In fact, he was determined to fire me. He constantly brought false accusations against me to the head pastor, then turned around and told me the senior pastor was against me but that he was standing up for me. This caused constant strife between the head pastor and myself. My supervisor sent various reprimanding memos to the staff, none mentioning my name but all bearing such a striking resemblance to me that all who read them recognized that the paper trail always pointed to me.

Months passed, and there seemed no way to alleviate my dilemma. It had escalated to the point where I had no contact with the senior pastor. This supervisor was attacking other employees in the same way, so at least I had company. Nevertheless, my family lived under constant pressure, never certain if we'd remain or be forced out.

It was at this point that I received written evidence of a decision this man had made. It dealt with me and exposed his true motives. I gathered my evidence and was prepared to bring it to the senior pastor. But early the next morning I found myself wrestling in prayer. For forty-five minutes I tried to shake the uncomfortable feeling I had in my spirit. I reasoned, *God, this man has been dishonest and wicked. He needs to be exposed. He is a destructive force in this ministry. The pastor should know the way he really is!* I continued justifying my intentions, *Everything I am reporting is factual and documented, not emotional.*

Finally, in frustration I blurted out, "God, You don't want me to expose him, do You?" In answer the peace of God flooded my heart. I knew God did not want me to do anything. I shook my head in disbelief as I threw away the evidence. Later, I realized I had wanted to defend and avenge myself more than protect any ministry. I had reasoned myself into believing my motives were selfless. My information was on track, but my motives were not.

Time passed, and one day as I was praying outside of the church before office hours I saw this man pull up in his car. God told me to go to him and humble myself. Immediately I was defensive, "No Lord, he needs to come to me. He is the one causing all the problems." I continued to pray, but again I sensed the Lord's insistence. I had no desire to do this, so I knew it was God. I called him and went into his office. Because God had dealt with me I was able to, with all sincerity, ask for his forgiveness. I confessed that I had been critical and judgmental of him. He immediately softened, and we talked for an hour. From that day his attacks against me stopped.

Six months later, while I was ministering out of the country, all the wrong this man had done was exposed. It had nothing to do with me but with various other areas and individuals. What he had done was much worse than what I knew. He was immediately fired. Judgment had come but not by my hand. The very thing he tried to do to others happened to him. However, when it happened I was not happy; I was grieved for him and his family. I understood their pain because I had gone through the same pain at his hands.

After sharing this incident with Addison, I said, "Son, you have a choice. You can continue to stand up for yourself and remain under your teacher's judgment, or you can realize you have not responded to his accusations in a godly manner. Then you can go to your teacher and apologize for being disrespectful and resisting his authority."

Addison questioned, "Then what do I do when I'm blamed for something I didn't do?"

"Let God defend you," I answered. "Has it worked to defend yourself?"

Addison responded, "No, I want God to defend me."

The next day he went to his teacher and humbled himself. He asked the teacher to forgive him for challenging him whenever he was corrected.

The teacher forgave him, and the next week Addison was honored as the student of the week for that class. Addison never had another problem. He ended the year in the instructor's favor.

If a nine-year-old can humble himself and obey God's Word in a crisis, how much more should we? I think this illustrates why Jesus said:

> Therefore whoever humbles himself as this little child is the greatest in the kingdom of heaven.
>
> —Matthew 18:4

When we humble ourselves by obeying God's Word, then His favor, grace, and righteous judgment rest upon us. This attitude is hard to develop in our quick, convenient, and easy society. We are trained to lack the stamina required to endure patiently. God's deliverance always comes but often differently than how or when we expect. But with His deliverance comes great glory! Humility is the road to true and enduring success.

11

ARM YOURSELF

A CHRISTIAN WHO IS NOT PREPARED TO SUFFER IS COMPARABLE TO A SOLDIER WHO GOES TO WAR UNARMED.

I F WE ARE going to follow the Master, we must settle one main issue: those who obey God will suffer in this life.

> Therefore, since Christ suffered for us in the flesh, arm yourselves also with the same mind, for he who has suffered in the flesh has ceased from sin.
>
> —1 PETER 4:1

I know this scripture is not one you pull out of your promise box and quote daily. I can't imagine that I would find it mounted on many refrigerators, mirrors, or plaques in order to claim its benefit each time you see it. Yet it holds one of the greatest promises of the New Testament. It assures us that those who suffer as Christ suffered will cease from sin. They will come to complete spiritual maturity.

HOW WE GROW SPIRITUALLY

Just as a human being matures physically and mentally, a believer also matures spiritually. We begin our spiritual walk with Christ as babies (1 Pet. 2:2) and ideally progress from infancy to childhood and then to adulthood or maturity (Eph. 4:14; Heb. 5:14).

Physical growth progresses with the passage of time. You will never find a two-year-old who is six feet tall! You cannot hurry physical maturity because it is a function of time. You naturally grow at a predetermined rate that is tied to the passage of time.

Intellectual growth is not a function of time but of learning. If you are thirty years old and have yet to master the first-grade level of reading, you will not be able to comprehend the tenth-grade level. Conversely, there are twelve-year-olds who have completed their high school education.

Spiritual growth is not a function of time or learning. I am sorry to report there are people who have been saved for years who are still immature babies or children in the spirit. This even includes people well-versed in Scriptures and memorization. Their knowledge of the Word does not mean they are skilled in its application.

If spiritual growth was a function of learning scripture, the Pharisees would have been the most mature of Jesus' day. They could quote the first five books of the Bible from memory, yet they didn't recognize the Son of God as He cast out demons and raised the dead.

So what causes spiritual growth? We just read that those who suffer as Christ suffered have reached spiritual maturity. Is it a function of suffering? I know many who have suffered greatly in their Christian walk, yet they remain in the trenches of bitterness and despair. These are not the spiritually mature. Suffering in itself does not cause spiritual growth. Maturity is found through our obedience to God in the midst of suffering. This is what it means to suffer as Christ suffered.

> Though He [Jesus] was a Son, yet He learned obedience by the things which He suffered.
>
> —HEBREWS 5:8

The suffering Jesus experienced was the direct result of His obedience to the will of God. The course or flow of this world's system directly opposes the kingdom of God; therefore, when we obey God we move against the current. This automatically introduces conflict, which gives birth to persecution, affliction, and tribulation. Obedience in the midst of this conflict causes spiritual growth. Examine again the words of Peter.

> Therefore, since Christ suffered for us in the flesh, arm yourselves also with the same mind, for he who has suffered in the flesh has ceased from sin, that he no longer should live the rest of his time in the flesh for the lusts [desires] of men, but for the will of God.
>
> —1 PETER 4:1–2

Suffering after the pattern of Christ brings a believer to maturity. This kind of suffering is caused when we resist the will of man to submit to the will of God.

It is not the religious suffering of self-induced pain and neglect. It is not dying of a disease or lacking the finances to pay your bills. God receives no glory from these. This mentality has actually caused many to search for an opportunity to inflict themselves with suffering in order to feel worthy. They believe God is pleased if they make themselves suffer for Him. This perverts their relationship, causing it to be based on works and not grace.

We are to embrace the suffering Christ experienced. Jesus did not suffer because He was diseased and lacked money to pay His bills.

No, the suffering He experienced was to be tempted in every manner possible and yet remain obedient to His Father. He was "in all points tempted as we are, yet without sin" (Heb. 4:15).

We face resistance when our desire and the desire of those who influence us will to go one direction, but God wills another.

A Confrontation With the Master

Jesus and His disciples had come into the region of Caesarea Philippi. He questioned them as to who they thought He was. In answer, Peter boldly declared Jesus to be the Christ, the Son of the living God. Jesus affirmed Peter's revelation.

Immediately following this, Jesus told them He was going to Jerusalem, would suffer many things, be killed, and then rise again. This disturbed Peter, so he pulled Jesus aside and rebuked Him.

> "Far be it from You, Lord; this shall not happen to You!" But He turned and said to Peter, "Get behind Me, Satan! You are an offense to Me, for you are not mindful of the things of God, but the things of men."
>
> —Matthew 16:23

Jesus had told His disciples that it was God's will that He suffer, die, and rise again. Yet Peter and the other disciples believed it was only a matter of time before Jesus set up His kingdom (Acts 1:6). They had all endured so much hardship to follow Jesus. Why would He die now when the hope of the kingdom was so near?

Peter was confused. *What does He mean, "I am going to die"? What will happen to us? What good could His dying possibly do?*

His fears focused on self-preservation instead of the will of the Father. He had yielded to the desires of the same selfish nature that entered man at the fall. It is the self-ruled will that opposes the will of God. Jesus seized the opportunity and used Peter's error to teach the disciples this powerful truth:

If anyone desires to come after Me, let him deny himself, and take up his cross, and follow Me. For whoever desires to save his life will lose it, but whoever loses his life for My sake will find it.

—MATTHEW 16:24–25

The only way to walk with Jesus is to completely deny yourself and take up the cross. This means dying to your own desire and will. This attitude enables you to follow Christ in His example of obedience in the face of suffering.

Whether you have died to your desires or not, you will eventually find yourself in a position where you will have to choose between comfort, advantage, security, self-esteem, or pleasure, and the will of God.

GOD DOES TEST US

God purposely steers us to these places where we must choose between our desire and His will. It is called His testing. In Psalm 11:5 we find, "The LORD tests the righteous." And again in Psalm 17:3, "You have tested my heart... You have tried me and have found nothing; I have purposed that my mouth shall not transgress." Paul affirms this with, "We speak, not as pleasing men, but God who tests our hearts" (1 Thess. 2:4).

Abraham waited twenty-five years for his son of promise. This in itself was a test. Most people will not wait more than a few months for the promise of God. After Isaac was born, God waited until Abraham and he were very close before He gave Abraham another test.

Now it came to pass after these things that God tested Abraham, and said to him, "Abraham!" And he said, "Here I am." Then He said, "Take now your son, your only son Isaac, whom you love, and go to the land of Moriah, and offer him there as a burnt offering on one of the mountains of which I shall tell you."

—GENESIS 22:1–2

Notice the scripture specifically says, "God tested Abraham." Isaac was more dear than life to Abraham. Yet Abraham proved his love for God by offering his most precious possession. Abraham rose early in the morning and made the three-day journey to the place God showed him. He bound his son on the altar and raised the knife in obedience to God. Then the angel of the Lord said:

> Do not lay your hand on the lad, or do anything to him; for now I know that you fear God, since you have not withheld your son, your only son, from Me.
>
> —Genesis 22:12

Joseph Passed the Test

Let's look again at Abraham's great-grandson Joseph. God gave him a dream of leadership. God knew beforehand exactly how it would come to pass—Joseph's older brothers would turn on him and sell him into slavery. The Lord did not panic when his jealous brothers did this wicked thing. He knows the end from the beginning (Isa. 46:10). God did not author their evil behavior, but He did use the opportunity it afforded to test Joseph's heart.

> He [God] sent a man before them—
> Joseph—who was sold as a slave.
> They hurt his feet with fetters,
> He was laid in irons.
> Until the time that his word came to pass,
> The word of the Lord tested him.
>
> —Psalm 105:17–19

Joseph did not disobey or dishonor God. He believed in the dream, but even more he believed in the God who had promised it. God's promise was so real that Joseph clung to it in the midst of unbelief and adversity. He believed yet suffered. His obedience was accompanied by suffering. He faced the same temptation his descendants would later face in the wilderness. Would he complain, be offended and bitter toward God and his brothers, or would he learn obedience by that which he suffered? He chose obedience and endured suffering because he knew God was faithful. In the end he was greatly rewarded for faithfulness.

A DIFFERENT HEART

Joseph's descendants (the people of Israel) were also tested numerous times. But they had a different heart than what Joseph had. Over and over they failed and chose their own comfort, security, and pleasure over God's heart.

They were first tested when Pharaoh would not let them go, even after he'd seen the miracles. Because of the hardness of Pharaoh's heart, things got much worse for them. They were no longer supplied with straw for their quota of bricks. This meant that after a long day of toiling under the hot Egyptian sun they had to glean in the fields by night. In the face of this hardship, they complained to Moses (Exod. 5:6–21).

Later, after even mightier signs and wonders, Moses encouraged the people to believe God's promise of deliverance. But "they did not heed Moses, because of anguish of spirit and cruel bondage" (Exod. 6:9). It seemed the more God's plan was revealed, the worse it was for the descendants of Abraham. They were so discouraged they wanted to forget their dream of freedom and embrace Egyptian slavery. The pressure of their circumstances caused them to be mindful of the things of men rather than the plan of God.

When they left Egypt, God led them right up to the Red Sea where He once again hardened Pharaoh's heart so that Pharaoh pursued them. Now there was a sea before them and behind them a massive army waiting to butcher them. Watch the response of the Israelites.

> Then they said to Moses, "Because there were no graves in Egypt, have you taken us away to die in the wilderness? Why

have you so dealt with us, to bring us up out of Egypt? Is this not the word that we told you in Egypt, saying, 'Let us alone that we may serve the Egyptians?' For it would have been better for us to serve the Egyptians than that we should die in the wilderness."

—Exodus 14:11–12

Notice the words, "it would have been better for us." This is a key statement; it revealed their disobedient hearts. They were more concerned about themselves than the will of God. This is exactly what Jesus was saying to Peter when He said, "You are not mindful of the things of God, but the things of men" (Matt. 16:23). The only way we can fulfill the will of God is to lay down our lives and trust in His loving care for us. If not, we will abort His will whenever we perceive the suffering as more difficult than we can bear.

Even though they complained, God delivered Abraham's descendants by parting the Red Sea. They crossed over on dry ground and turned to watch those who had oppressed them for four centuries buried under the waters.

After seeing all this, Israel sang and danced with great joy. Oh the love and confidence they had for God now that they had seen Him move so mightily on their behalf. They would never doubt Him again! Right? Wrong!

A mere three days later God presented them with a new test.

So Moses brought Israel from the Red Sea; then they went out into the Wilderness of Shur. And they went three days in the wilderness and found no water. Now when they came to Marah, they could not drink the waters of Marah, for they were bitter...And the people complained against Moses.

—Exodus 15:22–24

Complaining is a form of rebellion. It murmurs that God's way is not the right way, His provision not good enough. Just three days after they saw God's mighty power they failed another test. Even so,

God provided the water they needed.

A few days later the people complained again because they were short of food. Disgruntled they murmured about how much better their food had been back in Egyptian slavery.

God told Moses, "Behold, I will rain bread from heaven for you. And the people shall go out and gather a certain quota every day, that I may test them" (Exod. 16:4).

This pattern of testing and rebellion repeated itself many times. Their constant rebellion caused them to never leave their place of testing. Hebrews sums up the sad story.

> The Holy Spirit warns us to listen to him, to be careful to hear his voice today and not let our hearts become set against him, as the people of Israel did. They steeled themselves against his love and complained against him in the desert while he was testing them. But God was patient with them forty years, though they tried his patience sorely; he kept right on doing his mighty miracles for them to see. "But," God says, "I was very angry with them, for their hearts were always looking somewhere else instead of up to me, and they never found the paths I wanted them to follow."
>
> —HEBREWS 3:7–10, TLB

PREPARATION FOR THE KINGDOM

"Their hearts were always looking somewhere else." This is the behavior of an individual who has elevated comfort over obedience. They will follow God into the easy places only to turn aside as the path becomes difficult. *Surely this is not God,* they assure themselves as the road takes a turn toward hardship. Their hearts may know this is the road God has for them, but they allow their minds to talk them out of it, asserting, "God wants me happy, at peace, and prosperous."

Hear what Paul has to say to the young churches in Lystra, Iconium and Antioch. He had returned to them to strengthen the souls of these new disciples. How did he accomplish this? He exhorted them with,

Enemy Access Denied

"We must through many tribulations enter the kingdom of God" (Acts 14:22). Those who love "the good life" would question his statement, asking in disbelief, "Is that supposed to strengthen me?"

Hear again what the Holy Spirit spoke through Paul to the Thessalonian believers.

> We are happy to tell other churches about your patience and complete faith in God, in spite of all the crushing troubles and hardships you are going through. This is only one example of the fair, just way God does things, for he is using your sufferings to make you ready for his kingdom.
>
> —2 Thessalonians 1:4–5, TLB

This body of believers is commended by Paul. Today would we consider the hardships a sign of weak faith? Notice the statement, "He is using your sufferings to make you ready for His kingdom." Just as Jesus did, we learn obedience by what we suffer. This prepares us for His kingdom because spiritual growth progresses as we obey in the midst of suffering. This lends understanding to Paul's letter to the Philippian believers.

> For to you it has been granted on behalf of Christ, not only to believe in Him, but also to suffer for His sake.
>
> —Philippians 1:29

I was a believer for years before I recognized this scripture. I had passed over it many times because I did not believe in suffering. It did not fit my doctrine, so I omitted it. In my eyes all who suffered were either in sin or had not developed their faith. How immature!

When God opened my eyes to this truth, I had to laugh. Paul presents suffering as if it were a great honor or promise. "For to you it has been granted." You wonder, *What wonderful blessing has been granted to me?* Excited, you continue to read but then discover, "to suffer for His sake." What does Paul mean by "granted"? Is that a promise? Sounds more like a discouraging report!

But in fact, it is a promise because we are "heirs of God and joint heirs with Christ, if indeed we suffer with Him, that we may also be glorified together" (Rom. 8:17). Those who suffer with Him will be glorified with Him. How do we suffer with Him? Paul amplifies this in his letter to the Colossians.

> [Even] now I rejoice in the midst of my sufferings on your behalf. And in my own person I am making up whatever is still lacking and remains to be completed [on our part] of Christ's afflictions, for the sake of His body which is the church.
> —Colossians 1:24, amp

Paul had a strong understanding of suffering in his life because of the way the Lord called him into ministry. Paul received his calling from God through a man, Ananias, who prayed for him to receive his sight after his experience on the road to Damascus. Ananias was told, "Go, for he is a chosen vessel of Mine...For I will show him how many things he must suffer for My name's sake" (Acts 9:15–16). God prepared Paul for suffering from the very onset of his ministry. The Holy Spirit does the same for us by His Word.

> For even to this were you called [it is inseparable from your vocation]. For Christ also suffered for you, leaving you [His personal] example, so that you should follow in His footsteps.
> —1 Peter 2:21, amp

I Take Pleasure

You can understand Paul's final heart cry: "That I may know Him and the power of His resurrection, and the fellowship of His sufferings, being conformed to His death" (Phil. 3:10). The word *fellowship* means "participation with." Paul longed to participate with Christ in His sufferings, for he came to understand that in Christ's sufferings he found intimacy with Jesus.

In his earlier years Paul asked God to remove one of the hardships he was experiencing. He had yet to understand the purpose godly suffering played (2 Cor. 12:7–9). Later he understood its purpose. Then Paul no longer requested a life free of suffering. "So for the sake of Christ, I am well pleased and take pleasure in infirmities, insults, hardships, persecutions, perplexities and distresses; for when I am weak [in human strength], then am I [truly] strong (able, powerful in divine strength)" (2 Cor. 12:10, AMP).

Notice he said, "I am well pleased and take pleasure." Did he really say that? Yes, he had been caught up beyond the interest of self and had glimpsed the glory beyond hardship. That is why he could say to the Romans, "For I consider that the sufferings of this present time are not worthy to be compared with the glory which shall be revealed in us" (Rom. 8:18). Who is this us he referred to? All who have suffered as Christ.

Hear this wonderful promise:

> Beloved, do not think it strange concerning the fiery trial which is to try you, as though some strange thing happened to you; but rejoice to the extent that you partake of Christ's sufferings, that when His glory is revealed, you may also be glad with exceeding joy.
>
> —1 Peter 4:12–13

If you look closely at these verses, you see that the greater the trial, the more you should proportionately rejoice. You will also notice that the extent to which you suffer with Christ's sufferings is the extent to which His glory will be revealed. This explains why the disciples rejoiced in their trials: they looked beyond the hardship into the realm of glory.

Those who rejoice in the furnace come out of the furnace. Those who murmur in the wilderness die in the wilderness. The children of Israel could not see beyond the desert. Joshua and Caleb saw past the suffering of the desert into the Promised Land of milk and honey.

Settle it in your heart that there will be hardships in serving the Lord. We do not need to look for opportunities to suffer. But as we live obedient to God they will present themselves. We are forewarned in this:

> Many are the afflictions of the righteous.
>
> —PSALM 34:19

Yet there is no defeat in the suffering of Christ! For the psalmist continued:

> But the LORD delivers him out of them all.
>
> —PSALM 34:19

Paul affirmed this:

> But thanks be to God, who gives us the victory through our Lord Jesus Christ.
>
> —1 CORINTHIANS 15:57

ARM YOURSELF

Often our flesh will not be pampered as we obey God.

Jesus made it clear that to follow Him, there must be a denying of self by taking up the cross of death to self. Look again at our theme verse for this chapter.

> Therefore, since Christ suffered for us in the flesh, arm your-selves also with the same mind, for he who has suffered in the flesh has ceased from sin.
>
> —1 PETER 4:1

A Christian who is not prepared to suffer is comparable to a soldier who goes to war unarmed! Can you imagine the United States sending our men to war without training and weapons? They would fail! Unarmed soldiers are either killed, captured, or severely wounded, unless they desert the battle and their duty, thereby accomplishing nothing. That's why Peter said, "Arm yourself."

Christians who are not armed to suffer respond to trials, afflictions, and persecutions with shock, bewilderment, or amazement. In this state of stupor they will react to the situation at hand as opposed to following the lead of their Commander.

Let me give you an example of one who is armed. A crucial part of training for airline pilots comes through the use of flight simulators. In these simulators pilots are confronted by almost every flight emergency they might face. In the safety of this setting they hone their response skills until they successfully face each situation. This arms them for emergencies. When something happens on an actual flight, they do not panic. They respond calmly, assisted by their extensive training. Even though the passengers may panic and give way to shock and hysteria, the pilot remains calm and in full control. Investigators who review black box tape recordings from crashes are amazed by the calmness of pilots. There is no panic in their voices even up to the moment of the crash. They are armed!

Jesus rebuked Peter for being mindful of the things of men. At that time Peter was not armed to suffer. Jesus was. This is confirmed by Luke 9:51, "Now it came to pass, when the time had come for Him to be received up, that He steadfastly set His face to go to Jerusalem." He would not be distracted from His course of obedience. He was unshakable in His resolve.

His twelve followers had quite a different perspective. Undoubtedly they were not armed to suffer.

> Now they were on the road, going up to Jerusalem, and Jesus was going before them; and they were amazed. And as they followed they were afraid. Then He took the twelve aside again and began to tell them the things that would happen to Him.
>
> —Mark 10:32

They were amazed! In shock! Their thoughts ran wild with fear: *How can He head toward Jerusalem, knowing what awaits Him there? I can understand that He knows He is destined to die, but I can't comprehend embracing it. Maybe it is just a possibility and will not happen.*

Their thoughts were interrupted as Jesus pulled them aside to remind them He was going to Jerusalem to die. They were amazed and confused. Again their thoughts mocked them, *I don't understand. What good could this do anyone?*

Jesus was steadfast in His obedience; the disciples wavered in shock and uncertainty. Our maturity level is revealed in difficult times. How we handle persecution, tribulation, and other forms of hardship is a gauge for our true level of spirituality.

Jesus fulfilled His Father's will, yet not without a battle. The night before His crucifixion, He had to resist the temptation to preserve Himself. Under the pressure of this war He shed drops of blood (Matt. 26:36–44; Luke 22:44; Heb. 12:3–4). We are told, "He humbled Himself and became obedient to the point of death, even the death of the cross" (Phil. 2:8). He humbled Himself and therefore was given grace from His Father to endure the suffering required by obedience. He endured the most awful and gruesome death known to mankind.

HE IS OUR EXAMPLE

If we are to follow Jesus' example (1 Pet. 2), we must arm ourselves in the same manner. Paul did so. He shared his armor with his disciples, the elders of Ephesus.

> And see, now I go bound in the spirit to Jerusalem, not knowing the things that will happen to me there, except that the Holy Spirit testifies in every city, saying that chains and tribulations await me.
>
> —ACTS 20:22–23

How would we respond to prophetic words of persecution, hardship, and tribulation awaiting us at each turn? I am not implying that every genuine word from God should be of this nature, but there needs to be a balance.

A lot of our preaching and prophetic words have encouraged the wrong attitude in many believers. Our messages have been nice, comfortable, happy, or exciting. Our prophecies foretell prosperity and peace, all will be well. This encourages people to seek God for what He can do for them. The foundation of their love for Him shifts from who He is to what He can provide. They seek to fulfill the prophecy rather than obey the God of the prophecy. They are not interested in magnifying Jesus, whether by life or death (Phil. 1:20). They want their promise! They are not armed to suffer.

Many people surrounding Paul urged him not to go to Jerusalem because that was where it was prophesied he would suffer. However, Paul knew that Jerusalem was his directive from God. He declared that he would go no matter what happened.

> But none of these things move me; nor do I count my life dear to myself, so that I may finish my race with joy, and the ministry which I received from the Lord Jesus, to testify to the gospel of the grace of God.
>
> —ACTS 20:24

Notice he was armed to suffer, and this gave him the ability to finish his race with joy. Many never start or complete their race because they are not prepared or because the way appears too difficult. It is like trying to run a marathon without ever training.

Some will be saved, but they will pass through fire first (1 Cor. 3:15). They had chosen to believe the wrong messages. They wanted preaching that would encourage them in their comfort. Tears shed at the judgment seat of Christ are extremely painful; they are shed in the light of the knowledge of what could have been if the course of obedience had been completed.

There are those who will finish their race with great joy. These are the overcomers—overcoming by the blood of the Lamb and the word of their testimony. They will not love their lives unto the death (Rev. 12:11).

Overcome! Let this be your aim, your goal and your testimony.

12

THE BLESSINGS OF OBEDIENCE

GOD GIVES HIS HOLY SPIRIT TO THOSE WHO OBEY HIM (ACTS 5:32).

A

T THIS POINT we now turn our focus to the wonderful blessings of obedience. This will be most enjoyable. Yes, there is
suffering in obeying God, but it does not compare with the blessings
of obedience! This was the reason why the imprisoned Paul and Silas
could sing hymns in the night (Acts 16:25). They saw beyond their
hardship and glimpsed the glory.

More than one book could be written just expounding the benefits of walking in obedience to God. As you have seen, this was not
the direction God had for this book. Though we will cover some

benefits, you are destined to discover a multitude through your continued study and experiences in Christ.

I believe God's mandate for this book was instruction and warning—instruction on how to walk in obedience and warning to keep from deception. Instruction and warning are more crucial than the outlining of the benefits, for when you walk in the counsel and wisdom of God, you automatically experience the benefits, even if you are unaware of them. Conversely, you could know all the benefits and never receive them if you are not grounded in God's instruction and warning.

Increase Our Faith

A few months before I began this book, I had come into our ministry offices at 5:30 a.m. to pray and read my Bible. I like this time of day because there are no interruptions. I had opened my Bible to one of the New Testament epistles, but before I could read a word, the Lord spoke, "Turn in your Bible to Luke 17:5." My excitement rose, for I knew from experience that any time God has done this it was to show me something specific. I quickly flipped over to the scripture.

> And the apostles said to the Lord, "Increase our faith."
>
> —Luke 17:5

My thoughts immediately turned along these lines: *OK, God is going to speak to me about faith.* I had read this passage several times and had even preached from it. I knew what was coming in the next few verses. Still there was an excitement as I continued, searching each line for His hidden treasure. I was surprised to find God was not speaking to me about faith at all but on the subject of obedience. Continue with me:

> So the Lord said, "If you have faith as a mustard seed, you can say to this mulberry tree, 'Be pulled up by the roots and be planted in the sea,' and it would obey you."
>
> —Luke 17:6

This illustrates that faith is given to each and every believer as a mustard seed. It is the kingdom principle of seedtime and harvest. "The kingdom of God is as if a man should scatter seed on the ground" (Mark 4:26). When we were saved we were allotted a measure of faith (Rom. 12:3). This faith is in seed form.

The apostles asked the Lord to increase their faith. But from what He is about to show them we learn it is our responsibility to increase our faith. Listen to this parable He uses to explain how to increase our faith:

> And which of you, having a servant plowing or tending sheep, will say to him when he has come in from the field, "Come at once and sit down to eat"? But will he not rather say to him, "Prepare something for my supper, and gird yourself and serve me till I have eaten and drunk, and afterward you will eat and drink"? Does he thank that servant because he did the things that were commanded him? I think not.
>
> —LUKE 17:7–9

This parable always puzzled me. Why did Jesus go from comparing faith to a seed over to a servant plowing, tending sheep, and making dinner for his master? I did not understand until the morning God revealed it to me in my office.

First, let's remember what question He is answering by this parable. It could be paraphrased, "How do we increase this seed of faith?" Next, examine the major focus of the parable. It represents the obedience of a servant toward his master. Referring to the servant's actions Jesus said, "He did the things that were commanded him."

A servant is responsible to carry out completely the will of his master, not just a portion or a sampling of it. It represents taking a task from start to completion. How often do many people begin a project or assignment never to finish it because they lost interest or because the labor and suffering became too intense? The true and faithful servant completes the project. He not only works the fields, but he also brings the fruit of his labor to his master and prepares the meal. This represents true obedience.

Let's recall two very important points.

1. We must grow spiritually in the grace of God.
2. We grow through obedience!

So how does this seed of faith grow in our hearts? By now you probably know the answer—by obedience—not partial and occasional obedience but obedience performed faithfully and diligently. Look closely at what Jesus went on to say.

> So likewise you, when you have done all those things which you are commanded, say, "We are unprofitable servants. We have done what was our duty to do."
>
> —LUKE 17:10

His answer emphasizes two aspects of increasing faith. First, obedience to completion: "when you have done all those things which you are commanded." Second, humility toward God: "We are unprofitable servants. We have done what was our duty to do."

Obedience is not obedience until we have completed all that we have been told to do. In addition, our posture of humility keeps us in His grace. Both of these things foster an atmosphere for faith to grow. Jesus used this parable to explain that faith increases as we submit to God's authority. The greater our submission to God, the greater our faith!

Jesus is teaching His disciples, "Pursue true humility, which will keep you in the grace of God. That grace will give you the ability to walk in obedience. By submitting to God's authority and walking in complete obedience your faith will increase."

GREAT FAITH

Then the Holy Spirit reminded me of the Roman centurion who came to Jesus for help (Matt. 8). I quickly turned in my Bible to read this account afresh. As Jesus entered Capernaum, a centurion came to Him, pleading for Jesus to heal his servant who was at home in bed, paralyzed and racked with pain.

"Yes," Jesus said, "I will come and heal him."

But the centurion restrained Him by saying, "Lord, I am not worthy that You should come under my roof. But only speak a word, and my servant will be healed." Now read carefully why this soldier could say this to Jesus.

> For I also am a man under authority, having soldiers under me. And I say to this one, "Go," and he goes; and to another, "Come," and he comes; and to my servant, "Do this," and he does it.
>
> —MATTHEW 8:9

This Roman soldier had a greater understanding of authority and obedience than most. He knew that those who were submitted to authority could be entrusted authority of their own. He was saying to Jesus, "I recognize You're a man under God's authority just as I am under the governing authority of my commanding officer. Because I obey my commander, I have been entrusted with those under my authority. Therefore, I have but to say one word, and the soldiers under me instantly obey."

He understood Jesus' source of authority. He recognized that Jesus' authority came from God. He knew Jesus was totally submitted to the Father. He knew this meant that all Jesus needed to do was speak a word and the devils who tormented his servant had to obey. Notice Jesus' response to this man's understanding of submission to authority.

> When Jesus heard it, He marveled, and said to those who followed, "Assuredly, I say to you, I have not found such great faith, not even in Israel!"
>
> —MATTHEW 8:10

Notice Jesus linked directly faith and submission. This Roman soldier displayed greater faith than anyone in Israel because of his honor, respect, and submission to authority.

The centurion said, "All you have to do is speak a word and the tormentor will leave." Now tie this in with what Jesus said to the disciples who desired increased faith: "If you have faith as a mustard seed, you can say to this mulberry tree, 'Be pulled up by the roots and be planted in the sea,' and it would obey you" (Luke 17:6). Notice Jesus said all you have to do is speak a word and the tree will obey you! Who does this mulberry tree obey? The one who "did the things that were commanded him" (Luke 17:9–10).

I have watched believers who were insubordinate to God's authority have a rough time. They are either barely making it or fighting to survive, not just in finances but in all areas—their marriage, children, Christian walk, and so on. They talk a good talk and may even pray fervently, yet deep down they wonder why their faith is not stronger. It is evident their faith is weak because they are afraid to submit to God's authority.

I also have witnessed submitted believers who possessed simple yet great faith. They usually do not stand out, for they are humble. Yet their words ring with the authority of heaven, and when things are rough, they shine bright.

God Reveals Himself to the Obedient

We are required to live by faith, for "without faith it is impossible to please Him...For by it the elders obtained a good testimony" (Heb. 11:6, 2). Just like these elders of old, we receive the promises of God through faith and patience (Heb. 6:12). The greater our faith, the greater the capacity for us to receive God's promise. Our faith increases as our obedience continues. We see this in the life of Abraham.

> By faith Abraham, when he was tested, offered up Isaac, and he
> who had received the promises offered up his only begotten son.
> —Hebrews 11:17

Abraham's obedience was complete. He did not reason himself out of obeying God's command. He did not procrastinate but rose early the morning after receiving the command. He undertook a difficult three-day journey to God's appointed place. Then he bound his son and lifted his knife, ready to slay his long-awaited promise.

While meditating on this God spoke to me, "Don't put Ishmael on the altar!" Ishmael was the son that Abraham conceived with Sarah's handmaiden, though the Lord had said earlier that Sarah would be the one to bear the promised son to Abraham. Ishmael represents what you have accomplished in your own strength. It is our attempt to bring to pass God's promise. Isaac represents the promise of God, the one you have waited and longed for. God will not ask for our Ishmael but for Isaac in His test of obedience.

After the angel of the Lord restrained Abraham from sacrificing his son, look what happens as a result of his obedience:

> Then Abraham lifted his eyes and looked, and there behind him was a ram caught in a thicket by its horns. So Abraham went and took the ram, and offered it up for a burnt offering instead of his son. And Abraham called the name of the place, The-Lord-Will-Provide.
>
> —Genesis 22:13–14

God revealed Himself in a new way to Abraham, *Jehovah-Jireh*. Abraham was the first to receive this revelation of God's character, which means: "Jehovah Sees."

God was not revealed to Abraham as "Jehovah Sees" until Abraham passed the test of obedience. There are many who claim to know the different characteristics of God's nature, yet they have never experienced obeying Him in the hard places. They may sing, "Jehovah Jireh, my provider," but it is a song from their heads not their hearts. They have yet to venture to the hard and arid place where He reveals Himself.

Not only did Abraham receive a fresh revelation of God's nature but he also secured, by his obedience, the promise God made to him. After he passed this test God told him:

> In your seed all the nations of the earth shall be blessed, because you have obeyed My voice.
>
> —Genesis 22:18

This is quite a different outcome than the one experienced by his descendants who died in the wilderness. They too were given a promise, but they never received it because of their insubordinate hearts.

A Test of Obedience

I entered the full-time ministry in 1983, leaving behind a good position as a mechanical engineer with Rockwell International to serve in the ministry of helps at a large church. One function of my job was transporting guest speakers and caring for their needs.

It was a step of obedience, and we saw God's blessing on it. It was evident we had moved up to a new level of faith where we had not walked before. At that level I found gifts of abilities and wisdom I had not previously possessed.

In the second month in this position, I enjoyed the honor of transporting a great international evangelist who had seen millions saved throughout the nations of the world. We immediately became close friends. He gave me his home phone number and encouraged me to call any time, so over the next four years I kept in touch with him. He came to the church once or twice a year, and we exchanged letters and phone calls. We were the same physical stature, and he gave me a complete wardrobe of his clothes. He invited us to visit him and his wife any time. It seemed he was as drawn to me as I was to him.

I knew I was called to preach the gospel to the nations of the world. It was one of God's promises to me. As time passed, my desire to work for this man grew. The more time I spent with him, the more I wanted to serve him. I frequently was approached by other believers who said, "I believe you will work for that man one day." This always brought me great excitement, for it was the desire that already burned in my heart. I was certain it would prove to be God's way of fulfilling His promise that I would preach the gospel to the nations. But for the time being I remained a van driver with big God-given dreams.

After I had worked for four years in this position, I shared with my pastor and his wife that I felt God was preparing us for a move. They supported us but also gave me the freedom to work for them as long as I wanted.

Eight hours after our meeting, the international evangelist called my home. He asked Lisa and me to come and oversee a local church and Bible school he was starting. He said, "John, can you see the vision? You'll start the church here in the United States and then start others like it all over the world where my wife and I have preached."

When I hung up the phone after our two-hour talk, I was so excited I just hit the ceiling. I went outside to think and drink in all that had just happened. It was almost too good to believe. As I walked outside, I noticed an uncomfortable feeling deep in my heart. I thought, *God, You can't be saying no.* I could not believe what was happening, so I tried to shake it off.

But the check in my spirit did not leave. I wrestled with it for three days, reasoning that it could not be from God. Finally in frustration I did an ignorant thing: thinking it was possible that I was battling the enemy, I shouted, "I am going to work for him in Jesus' name." The uncomfortable check in my spirit left.

Three weeks later, we flew to their headquarters and interviewed for five hours. We accepted the position and were introduced to their staff during their Christmas banquet. The salary was set, and we had a place to live.

I returned to Dallas, resigned from my position, and prepared for our move. But with only three weeks left before we were to leave, the uncomfortable witness in my spirit returned. Thank God for His mercy.

We flew again to their headquarters. This time everything was different. The meeting was strained and uncomfortable for all. Together we concluded that it was not God's will. We said our good-byes, and I left, knowing we had obeyed God. But I felt empty and bewildered. I no longer had the dream that had encouraged me.

Over the next few days I wept frequently while in prayer. Confused, one morning I cried out to God, "Why did You ask me to put the dream You gave me on the altar?"

God immediately answered, "I wanted to see if you were serving the dream or Me." Instantly my sadness left. In that moment many questions were answered. Now I understood. Later God showed me that I had passed a test.

A few months later another internationally known pastor asked me to join his church staff. He wanted me to oversee his young people. I almost laughed as I thought, *I have turned down the greatest opportunity I could have imagined, and now I'm being offered this menial position.* (It's terrible, but that's what I thought. I desperately searched for a check in my spirit but found only peace.)

I knew it was God, and I accepted the position two days later. As soon as I accepted the call to go, joy and life sprang up in my soul. We packed up everything and moved.

At our first Sunday service the pastor announced my arrival on staff and invited me to speak to the congregation.

Before moving, I had been eager to preach but was not very good at it. In fact, just the year before I had lost a tape to one of my teaching series from a Sunday school class and wanted to replace it, so I asked my wife and her friend to be my congregation in our living room while I rerecorded it. Halfway through the message, they both fell asleep. Looking back now it is comical. I became so frustrated I wanted to wake them up, but I couldn't because I was recording the message. I preached the last half of my message to two sleeping women.

Now I was getting up in front of a few thousand. My wife prayed, "God, please don't let John embarrass himself." (She told me this later.)

When I took the microphone, the Spirit of God came on me, and within thirty seconds the entire congregation was on their feet, going wild. I knew my words were not my own, and I felt an authority

I had never known before. For the first time I sensed power in the words I spoke. I sensed a flame burning deep inside me.

When I sat down the people kept shouting. I was shaking under the influence of God's presence. It continued for several minutes. My wife looked at me in disbelief and said, "What happened to you? You are not the same man!" It happened again when I rose to speak in the second Sunday service.

The youth group grew from 60 to 250 young people in one week. I was preaching like a new man. My wife describes it this way, "When you crossed the state line to our new home, you became a different man."

The faith and anointing on my life had increased due to my obedience. I believe if I had gone to work for the first international minister, I would not have risen in faith, anointing, and authority to the spiritual level I did as youth pastor. We must remember, God gives His Holy Spirit to those who obey Him (Acts 5:32).

GOD BRINGS FORTH HIS PROMISES

I grew more over the next two years in that position than I had in the previous eight years. A year and a half later my pastor had a vision that he shared with the eleven pastors of his staff. The vision held three messages; one dealt with the United States; one with our local church; and one with one of his pastors.

He told us the portion that concerned the United States and the local church and then said, "God has shown me that one of you pastors is not going to be on our staff much longer. You will travel full time. That pastor is you, John Bevere."

As he spoke, the Spirit of the Lord came on me, and I wept. He said, "I don't know when it will happen; all I know is that it will."

Six months later, August 1989, I received seven invitations from all corners of the United States to preach in the same three-week span of time. I made an appointment to share it with my senior pastor.

"What do I do with these?" I asked.

He laughed and said, "I prophesied it; looks like you're leaving."

He and I planned my departure for the end of the year.

Over the next three months two different men from a foreign nation at two different times called me out and prophesied what God was getting ready to do. They did not know me or what had transpired in the last nine months. In fact, the youth heard it for the first time in one of those services. My pastor, my wife, and I were in awe of how the Spirit of God confirmed what He was doing.

A month before my salary stopped, I was a bit concerned. I only had two new invitations to minister (having already gone to the seven meetings that I had received earlier), one at the beginning of January and the other at the end of February. We had very little money, not even a third of our house payment for a month.

My pastor had blessed me with a letter of recommendation and the addresses of six hundred pastors. He encouraged me, "Do what you would like with this."

I addressed several envelopes when suddenly the Spirit of God questioned me, "What are you doing?"

I replied, "I am letting churches know that I am available."

He said, "You will get out of My will."

I replied, "But nobody knows me out there!"

He said, "I know you; trust Me!"

I threw out the envelopes. As I write this book seven years later, we still travel full time. We have never lacked a penny or a place to preach. We have never had to send out letters begging for financial support. Though at times it's been tight, God has always been faithful. He has led me to more than thirty states and several nations. God is true to His promises!

God continues to fulfill His promise to me. It always comes His way. With each step of obedience comes a new level of faith.

Obedience to our Father is the only way to go because of the following reasons:

1. It honors Him with the glory He deserves.

2. People's lives are truly changed.

3. Obeying His will increases faith and develops character.

4. It is the only source of life, joy, and peace.

5. There awaits an eternal reward for our obedience.

> For we must all appear before the judgment seat of Christ, that each one may receive the things done in the body, according to what he has done, whether good or bad.
>
> —2 CORINTHIANS 5:10

This judgment is not of sinners but of believers. Notice Paul said, "good or bad." For those who obey God's will, "each one's work will become clear; for the Day will declare it, because it will be revealed by fire; and the fire will test each one's work, of what sort it is. If anyone's work which he has built on it endures, he will receive a reward" (1 Cor. 3:13–14).

Our God is a consuming fire (Heb. 12:29). He is the one who tests each of our works. Fire will burn and devour that which does not endure. It will purify and refine that which does. Our motives, intentions, and works will be revealed in His glorious light. Those who have obeyed with a pure heart will be rewarded. On the other hand:

> If anyone's work is burned, he will suffer loss; but he himself will be saved, yet so as through fire.
>
> —1 CORINTHIANS 3:15

The way we will spend eternity is determined by our submission to His authority here. Nothing else matters, except to live a life of obedience to His will.

> So, dear brothers [and sisters], work hard to prove that you really are among those God has called and chosen, and then you will never stumble or fall away. And God will open wide the gates of heaven for you to enter into the eternal kingdom of our Lord and Savior Jesus Christ.
>
> —2 PETER 1:10–11, TLB

Enemy Access Denied

Those who are wise will shine like the brightness of the heavens, and those who lead many to righteousness, like the stars for ever and ever.

—Daniel 12:3, NIV

May the grace of our Lord Jesus Christ be with you both now and forever.

EPILOGUE

WHEN THE LORD first gave me in prayer the title to the first edition of this book—*The Devil's Door*—I didn't fully understand what it meant. Later as I was writing, I discovered how God had warned Cain that sin crouched at his door (Gen. 4–7). Suddenly the title made sense.

The final thought I'd like to leave with you is in regard to this door. We can choose one of four responses when sin comes knocking.

1. Blatant disobedience

Hear these scriptures:

> Those who sat in darkness and in the shadow of death, bound in affliction and irons—because they rebelled against the words of God, and despised the counsel of the Most High.
>
> —PSALM 107:10–11

> Nevertheless they were disobedient and rebelled against You, cast Your law behind their backs and killed Your prophets, who testified against them to turn them to Yourself; and they worked great provocations. Therefore You delivered them into the hand of their enemies, who oppressed them.
>
> —NEHEMIAH 9:26–27

The way of disobedience is hard!

2. Reasoning yourself into disobedience

> And He gave them into the hand of the Gentiles, and those who hated them ruled over them. Their enemies also oppressed them, and they were brought into subjection under their hand. Many times He delivered them; *but they rebelled in their counsel,* and were brought low for their iniquity.
>
> —PSALM 106:41–43, EMPHASIS ADDED

This pronouncement was preceded by a long list of the times Israel rebelled, including the time Saul kept livestock from a conquered people, though God had told him to destroy every living thing. (See 1 Samuel 15.) "They rebelled in their counsel," the scripture says. They reasoned in their thought process until they found justification in disobedience. Their reasoning cost them dearly, which is why we are admonished:

> For the weapons of our warfare are not physical [weapons of flesh and blood], but they are mighty before God for the overthrow and destruction of strongholds...

What are these strongholds?

... [Inasmuch as we] refute arguments and theories and reasonings and every proud and lofty thing that sets itself up against the [true] knowledge of God; and we lead every thought and purpose away captive into the obedience of Christ (the Messiah, the Anointed One).

—2 Corinthians 10:4–5, AMP

By way of reasoning, Eve ate the fruit of the tree of the knowledge of good and evil. This false line of reasoning has troubled mankind ever since.

3. Obedience with a bad attitude

If you are willing and obedient, you shall eat the good of the land.

—Isaiah 1:19

A slave obeys but usually without a willing heart. There is a passive rebellion in his obedience. If things were his way he would not obey. Balaam obeyed God's word, but his heart longed to receive Balak's blessing. This passive rebellion was eventually exposed.

4. Obedience with a willing heart

Unlike the slave, a servant obeys with a willing heart. Only those who are obedient and possess a willing attitude eat the good of the land.

If they obey and serve Him [God], they shall spend their days in prosperity, and their years in pleasures.

—Job 36:11

What a promise! Yet the prosperity and pleasure he speaks of supersedes the type the world pursues.

Moses, when he came of age, refused to be called the son of Pharaoh's daughter, choosing rather to suffer affliction with the

185

people of God than to enjoy the passing pleasures of sin, esteeming the reproach of Christ greater riches than the treasures in Egypt; for he looked to the reward. By faith he forsook Egypt, not fearing the wrath of the king; for he endured as seeing Him who is invisible.

—HEBREWS 11:24–27

Even Scripture acknowledges there is a season of pleasure in sin, but it is fleeting and transitory. The prosperity and pleasure the world seeks are selfish or self-gratifying and therefore only endure but a moment in the span of eternity. But the prosperity and pleasures enjoyed by God's obedient children are for the present and yet endure and expand into eternity. They cannot be taken away by man since they have been given by God.

God also promised as we fulfilled our obedience by casting down all reasoning and thoughts that exalt themselves against our obedience to God, we would be equipped and ready to punish all disobedience (2 Cor. 10:3-6). In other words, our authority against the enemy would increase. Glory to God!

It is my hope and prayer that you now have developed an appetite for obeying God. You will be disappointed by all but His perfect will. In conclusion I would like to pray with you and agree to see Jesus glorified in your life and family.

Father, in the name of Jesus, thank You for Your truth and word revealed in this book. I embrace Your wisdom and welcome it into my heart. Let me not only understand but also empower me to live this life You've called me to. Under Your grace I humble myself and acknowledge Jesus Christ as more than just my Savior but as my Lord and Master. Give me Your grace to live an obedient life. By this grace may I love, fear, and serve You more perfectly. May Your will alone stand in my life and not my own or the will of any other. Keep me strong that I may be found blameless when I stand before You. Glorify Your name in my life, family, and church. Thank You, Lord, for Your faithfulness. Amen.

*Now to Him who is able to keep you
from stumbling, and to present you faultless
before the presence of His glory with exceeding joy,
to God our Savior, who alone is wise, be glory
and majesty, dominion and power,
both now and forever. Amen.*

—Jude 24–25

NOTES

Chapter 4
The Mystery of Lawlessness

1. Jay P. Green Sr., ed., *A Literal Translation of the Bible* in *The Interlinear Bible,* 2d ed. (Peabody, MA: Hendrickson Publishers, 1986), 1 Sam. 15:23.

2. R. Laird Harris, ed., *Theological Wordbook of the Old Testament,* vol. 2 (Chicago, IL: Moody Bible Institute, 1980), 2044a.

Chapter 6
The Strength of Rebellion

1. Green, *A Literal Translation,* Ps. 106:15.

Chapter 8
Grace That Misleads

1. *Nave's Topical Bible* in PC Study Bible Version 3.1 (Seattle, WA: BibleSoft, 1993), s.v. "Raca."

Chapter 9
The Fight of Faith

1. Edward Viening, ed., *Zondervan Topical Bible* (Grand Rapids, WA: Zondervan, 1969), s.v. "Love Feast."

Chapter 10
Humility—The Road to Success

1. *The Full Life Study Bible,* "Introduction to 1 Corinthians" (Grand Rapids, MI: Zondervan, 1992).

2. *The Full Life Study Bible,* "Introduction to Ephesians."

3. *The Full Life Study Bible,* "Introduction to 1 Timothy."

4. *The Full Life Study Bible,* "Introduction to Philippians."

BOOKS BY JOHN

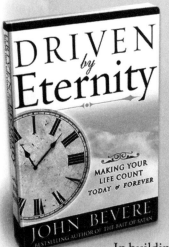

Driven by Eternity - hardback book
Making Your Life Count Today & Forever

In *Driven by Eternity*, John Bevere speaks to us about the compelling principles on how to live with hope and assurance that will carry us through to eternity.

Truth be told, most people would be left destitute if they prepared for their futures as carelessly as they've planned for eternity. Even believers often neglect this vital component of the Christian life. Often, we give little thought to what will happen beyond the end of today.

In building our lives to be ready for that Day of Judgment and maintaining an eternal frame of reference, we will develop significant lives. Learning to keep sight of the goal will allow us to begin laboring for rewards that endure—for eternity.

Please contact us today to receive your free copy of Messenger International's newsletter and our 32-page color catalog of ministry resources!

FREE NEWSLETTER & CATALOG

MESSENGER INTERNATIONAL

"Life-Transforming Truth"

The vision of MI is to strengthen believers, awaken the lost and captive in the church, and proclaim the knowledge of His glory to the nations. John and Lisa are reaching millions of people each year through television and by ministering at churches, Bible schools, and conferences around the world. We long to see God's Word in the hands of leaders and hungry believers in every part of the earth.

UNITED STATES
PO Box 888
Palmer Lake, CO 80133-0888
800-648-1477 (US & Canada)
Tel: 719-487-3000
Fax: 719-487-3300
E-mail: mail@messengerintl.org

EUROPE
PO Box 622
Newport, NP19 8ZJ
UNITED KINGDOM
Tel: 44 (0) 870-745-5790
Fax: 44 (0) 870-745-5791
E-mail: europe@messengerintl.org

AUSTRALIA
PO Box 6200
Dural, D.C. NSW 2158
AUSTRALIA
In AUS 1-300-650-577
Tel: +61 2 8850 1725
Fax +61 2 8850 1735
Email: australia@messengerintl.org

The *Messenger* television program broadcasts in 216 countries on
GOD TV, the Australian Christian Channel, and on the
New Life Channel in Russia. Please check your local listings for day and time.

WWW.MESSENGERINTL.ORG

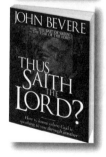